More From The Pastor's Desk

Rev. Alfred Flatten

ISBN-13: 978-1494474065

ISBN-10: 1494474069

A second collection of short teachings

From
The
Pastor's
Desk

With all my love and prayers for my grandchildren.

Contents:

A Love That Gives   6

A Total Revelation   12

Three Stages of Transformation   20

A Listening Heart   26

Between the Devil and the Deep Blue Sea   31

Becoming a "4H" Christian   38

Becoming a "4H" Christian – Part 2   44

Becoming a "4H" Christian – Part 3   50

Becoming a "4H" Christian – Part 4   54

That They May Have Life   60

Empowered   66

Six Ways to Grow in Assurance   71

Some Thoughts on Prayer   100

God's Book   108

The Power of Touch   114

Four Principles of Faith   121

Favoritism   125

Two Gifts of God   129

Second Chances   134

When He Reigns, It Pours   139

A Look at Change   148

I Want to Change, So Help Me God   153

The Knowledge of God   157

Word, Words, Words   167

Intentionally, On Purpose   176

"A Love That Gives"

1 John 2:9-11 – "Anyone who claims to be in the light but hates a brother or sister is still in the darkness. Anyone who loves their brother and sister lives in the light, and there is nothing in them to make them stumble. But anyone who hates a brother or sister is in the darkness and walks around in the darkness. They do not know where they are going, because the darkness has blinded them."

1 John 3:16-19 – "This is how we know what love is: Jesus Christ laid down his life for us. And we ought to lay down our lives for our brothers and sisters. If anyone has material possessions and sees a brother or sister in need but has no pity on them, how can the love of God be in that person? Dear children, let us not love with words or speech but with actions and in truth. This is how we know that we belong to the truth and how we set our hearts at rest in his presence:

I want to begin today by explaining the difference between "pity" and "compassion". Pity looks at the television screen and says; "Oh, those poor people" and feels sorry for them, and goes on with life. Compassion however, looks at the television screen with tear filled eyes, and says "I must do something to help!" Often we are not physically able to be there and provide personal help, but there are ways we can help. Compassion will surpass sympathy and do what - ever it can! Number one of course, we can pray. We can pray for God to somehow give wisdom as to providing for the needs of those affected. For those who are able, we can also provide by giving to those organizations like the Red Cross and others who provide disaster relief. We may feel that we can't do much, if anything personally or on an individual basis, but maybe there is something we can do together, as a church, as the body of Christ.

Well, let's get started; Once again, I am looking at John's letter of assurance. This is not a letter of condemnation or judgment, but rather a letter in which John gives us a list of things or ways in which we can point "inward" and KNOW that if these things are manifesting themselves in our lives, then we can be assured that we are a child of God; that we are born again; a part of the family of God, the body of Christ. If these things are not there in our lives, then John says we have a problem.

Brotherly love, as the title of this message suggests, is a love that gives. The command for God's people to love each other has been around since the Jewish Old Testament Law. Leviticus 19:18 says, "'Do not seek revenge or bear a grudge against one of your people, but love your neighbor as yourself. I am the LORD."

Jesus' command is for us to love each other in the way we saw him love us by going to the cross, and that's what made this command new when he told his friends at the last supper to "love each other, just as I have loved you." ...it is a sacrificial love...a love that puts others and their needs first. In John 13:34—Jesus said again; "A new command I give you: Love one another. As I have loved you, so you must love one another. By this all men will know that you are my disciples, if you love one another." Then he repeats it again in John 15:12—"My command is this: Love each other as I have loved you."

The terms "love" and "hate" are not necessarily emotions or feelings as much as attitudes; just as "light and darkness" are not places but rather actions that reflect our spiritual growth. The love we have for one another and for our neighbors is a love that expresses itself in our actions and attitudes, not our feelings. In fact, we are to love others whether we FEEL like it or not. Some people are easier to love than others; I heard one preacher say; "Some Christians are like porcupines...they've got a few good points, but they're hard to get close to!"

What does John mean here by hate? "He who hates his brother..." The dictionary tells us that hate is "a feeling of extreme hostility or extreme dislike of another." That suffices as far as the definition. We know well this feeling, this dislike, this aversion to someone, a sense of extreme hostility toward another. Yet, you and I need to understand that it can be expressed in two different ways. It can be active, in that we indulge in malicious talk or injurious actions toward another. We can strike them, or beat them, throw our garbage over their fence, or mistreat them in some way. We can attack them; we can slander them behind their back. All of these are active expressions of hate, and perhaps most of us think of hate only in this sense. But hate can also be expressed passively and still be hate. It can be expressed by indifference, by coldness, by isolation, by exclusion, and unconcern for others.

If you claim you are a child of God and yet "hate" any man - in John's sense of the word - because of his *face*, his *place,* or his *race,* you are walking in the darkness, and, may need to check your walk. Sure it's easy loving my wife, and loving my friends, but loving people I find irritating, people who I think are weird, or loving people who just grate me the wrong way; that takes God's love.

That's why the word John chooses here is the Greek word "agape", which describes God's kind of love, the kind of love that's given freely and generously, regardless of the worthiness of the object. C. S. Lewis was right when he wrote in Mere Christianity that "we spend too much time worrying about whether we really love our neighbor or not, when we should just act as if we do, and as we pray for them and do loving things, love will happen." When we give way to feelings and attitudes of hatred that John describes, we harden our own heart.

Our love for one another is our badge of identity as Christians. John is telling us the love we have is the badge that identifies us. When a police officer comes to your door, they will identify themselves by showing you their badge…when we claim to be saved, the badge people will see is the love - or lack there of - we have in our lives. If we cannot love other Christians…those of God's family, how are we going to love others who need to be in the family?

Agape love is a love that gives. "For God so loved the world that He gave…His only Son"…The love motivates the action. John says "If anyone has material possessions and sees his brother in need but has no pity on him, how can the love of God be in him? Dear children, let us not love with words or tongue, (pity is not enough) "That's too bad" or "I feel so sorry for you" won't cut it! But love with "actions and truth" in true compassion. We need to put hands and feet on our words if we are walking with our brother.

"Here then is the assurance" says John, if we see someone in need (and remember there are many types of needs) and we have the ability or the capability to help, even in the smallest way, and yet are not stirred by compassion to take action, how can we set our hearts at rest?

In Matthew 25:40 Jesus said; "Whatever you did for the least of these my brothers, you did for me." The point is that we did something out of love, agape' love, which tells us that we are not only walking in the light, but that we are truly walking with our brother.

Finally, look at 1 John chapter 4 verses 7-12 ...

"Dear friends, let us love one another, for love comes from God. Everyone who loves has been born of God and knows God. Whoever does not love does not know God, because God is love. This is how God showed his love among us: He sent his one and only Son into the world that we might live through him. This is love: not that we loved God, but that he loved us and sent his Son as an atoning sacrifice for our sins. Dear friends, since God so loved us, we also ought to love one another. No one has ever seen God; but if we love one another, God lives in us and *his love is made complete* in us.

I don't know how you would interpret that, but to me it says "If God's love stops here with me, it is incomplete! God's love is made complete when it flows through me and out to others! It's a love that gives. It gives of its time; it gives of its money; it gives of its talents and abilities; it serves without thought of reward.

However, there is a flip side to this coin; when we are willing to give, there must be a willingness to receive! We could say; "What good is it if we see a brother in need and we are willing to help, but he is not willing to receive? How many times do you suppose God has asked that question? He is so willing to freely give of everything He has…all His love, all his peace, all His joy, all His wisdom…and the abundant life that He desires for us to live; but, we are unwilling to receive it. What is stopping you from doing that today?

Scripture – John 4:1-30 – "Now Jesus learned that the Pharisees had heard that he was gaining and baptizing more disciples than John— although in fact it was not Jesus who baptized, but his disciples. So he left Judea and went back once more to Galilee.

Now he had to go through Samaria. So he came to a town in Samaria called Sychar, near the plot of ground Jacob had given to his son Joseph. Jacob's well was there, and Jesus, tired as he was from the journey, sat down by the well. It was about noon.

When a Samaritan woman came to draw water, Jesus said to her, "Will you give me a drink?" (His disciples had gone into the town to buy food.) The Samaritan woman said to him, "You are a Jew and I am a Samaritan woman. How can you ask me for a drink?" (For Jews do not associate with Samaritans) Jesus answered her, "If you knew the gift of God and who it is that asks you for a drink, you would have asked him and he would have given you living water."

"Sir," the woman said, "you have nothing to draw with and the well is deep. Where can you get this living water? Are you greater than our father Jacob, who gave us the well and drank from it himself, as did also his sons and his livestock?"

Jesus answered, "Everyone who drinks this water will be thirsty again, but whoever drinks the water I give them will never thirst. Indeed, the water I give them will become in them a spring of water welling up to eternal life."

The woman said to him, "Sir, give me this water so that I won't get thirsty and have to keep coming here to draw water."

He told her, "Go, call your husband and come back."

"I have no husband," she replied.

Jesus said to her, "You are right when you say you have no husband. The fact is, you have had five husbands, and the man you now have is not your husband. What you have just said is quite true."

"Sir," the woman said, "I can see that you are a prophet. Our ancestors worshiped on this mountain, but you Jews claim that the place where we must worship is in Jerusalem."

"Woman," Jesus replied, "believe me, a time is coming when you will worship the Father neither on this mountain nor in Jerusalem.

You Samaritans worship what you do not know; we worship what we do know, for salvation is from the Jews. Yet a time is coming and has now come when the true worshipers will worship the Father in the Spirit and in truth, for they are the kind of worshipers the Father seeks. God is spirit, and his worshipers must worship in the Spirit and in truth."

The woman said, "I know that Messiah" (called Christ) "is coming. When he comes, he will explain everything to us."

Then Jesus declared, "I, the one speaking to you—I am he."

Just then his disciples returned and were surprised to find him talking with a woman. But no one asked, "What do you want?" or "Why are you talking with her?"

Then, leaving her water jar, the woman went back to the town and said to the people, "Come, see a man who told me everything I ever did. Could this be the Messiah?" They came out of the town and made their way toward him."

Vs. 39-42 – "Many of the Samaritans from that town believed in him because of the woman's testimony, "He told me everything I ever did." So when the Samaritans came to him, they urged him to stay with them, and he stayed two days. And because of his words many more became believers. They said to the woman, "We no longer believe just because of what you said; now we have heard for ourselves, and we know that this man really is the Savior of the world."

In this text, Jesus is speaking to the woman at the well in Samaria, we are told, and in verse 23 He says "A time is coming and has now come when true worshipers will worship the Father in spirit and in truth, for they are the kind of worshipers the Father seeks".... God, the Father, seeks those who worship in spirit and in truth... I believe that to "worship in spirit" means that every part of our being is involved; body, mind, heart, and soul, all focused on the same thing at the same time. To worship in truth is to know God the Father

Almighty is who He says He is; it is to know that Jesus, the son of God, fully human and fully divine, was sent to be the only way of salvation and to reveal God and His kingdom to mankind; to worship in truth is to know that the Holy Spirit is how God chooses to convict, guide, teach and reach all who would come to Him. And, I think that when that happens, when we worship in spirit and in truth...every one of us knows...We know that God is in our presence and that we are in the presence of God! I think it is at those times when we experience the Holy Spirit moving in our midst, and the love, peace, mercy and grace of God are in abundance and fill the sanctuary!... I also know that when that experience does not happen...it's not God's fault!

That being said, I find in this story a sort of a progression of revelation as to who Jesus is...And, I also believe there is a parallel of this progression in us as worshipers...This progression takes place until we reach the point of worshiping in "spirit and in truth" in the full sense of the words, as we will see in this encounter at the well.

This woman sees Jesus, first of all as a man...as a Jewish man; then she sees him as a prophet; third, she sees him as the "Christ" or Messiah; and finally she sees him as her Savior.

The progression begins in verse 9 – The woman approaches the well, and Jesus says "Will you give me a drink?" She says to Jesus "You are a Jew and I am a Samaritan woman." This is important for several reasons. #1 it takes her by surprise, and she states the reason why "Jews do not associate with Samaritans." The study note in my Bible says "Jews believed that Samaritans were "unclean". The

Samaritans were racially mixed, they were religiously mixed, and the Jews would have nothing to do with Samaritans. This social and racial and religious segregation began way back in the time of Nehemiah and the return from captivity and the rebuilding of the walls in Jerusalem. It had been passed down from generation to generation…and Jesus – at this point in his ministry – and in the parable of the Good Samaritan – tries to break down those walls of separation.

But, the fact is that she recognizes Jesus as a man, a Jewish man. Jesus was not an angelic being who just appeared on the scene at age 30…We know from the Gospels that Jesus had a normal human birth… and grew up in a normal family with brothers and sisters. Jesus was fully human…He was a man.

There are people even today who recognize Jesus as a man. A Jewish man who lived some 2000 years ago…but, that's as far as their recognition goes. To many people He is no different than Mohammed, or Budda, or any other religious man that ever lived. As a man, he was also recognized as a good teacher, and a good leader among men, however, because of his death and resurrection from the dead, and the records of the Gospel writer's, we know that he was more than just a man.

Jesus peaks her curiosity by saying "If you knew the gift of God, and who it is that asks you for a drink, you would have asked him and he would have given you living water"… In other words, "If you really knew who I am, if you knew the power, the authority, the life changing things I could offer, I would give you living water!"

Within the hearts of men and women there is a thirst... a thirst for purpose, meaning, significance, satisfaction, a thirst for fulfillment. Sometimes we look for all the wrong things in all the wrong places to fill that thirst, and we find only stagnant waters. The water of the world and the flesh; the water of material things; the water of philosophy and pleasure is like the salt water of the Dead Sea...they only make us crave more. But, Jesus says "whoever drinks of the water I give him will never thirst"!

However, the first step in that process is recognizing our need. This woman was living an immoral life, and she needed to recognize her need for forgiveness. She needed to see the sin in her life for what it was, and why she needed what Jesus had to offer.

This is why Jesus calls the church to be "salt" and "light" in the world...because people need to see their need for the gift of salvation through Jesus Christ before they will come to Him.

In verse 19 – after Jesus points out her sin... she understands that he knows all about her and she says "I can see you are a prophet"...step two.

It seems to me that she didn't like the way the conversation was going, so she tries to change the subject; she brings up something that was somewhat of a "hot potato" in her day – whether or not they were to worship on this mountain or in Jerusalem? ... How many people today do the same thing? When they are confronted with the Gospel or religion or church, they turn the conversation to something like "Well, I don't think you have to be in a church to worship God! Or, "Well, what does *your* church believe about__?__and you fill in the blank with the hot potato of the day.

Jesus tells her that a time is coming when the place of worship will not matter... so, in a sense you could say that you don't have to be in church to worship God... But, then he rather bluntly tells her that the Samaritans worship "what they do not know". They did not really know God, and they had a limited view of the Messiah who was to come, and they had incorporated many pagan things into their worship...all in all, they had lost their heart for God because they got caught up in religion instead of a relationship! People still fall into that trap today!

True worship is not the music, or the style, or the buildings, or the programs, or anything else that is external. The heart of worship is...the HEART! While forms and locations and times, and styles, and traditions have their place, they are fruitless without hearts that have been filled with the living water that comes from Jesus Christ, the living Son of God!

Third, comes the revelation that Jesus is the Messiah. The Samaritans as well as the Jews knew that the scriptures spoke of one who was to come, but they were looking for a great teacher; a great leader; another Moses or Joshua or David to lead them... They were not looking for a Savior that would take upon himself the sins of the world and the eternal damnation of hell, and suffer and die, crucified on a Cross... You know, when you think about the revelation and the rise in power of the Anti-Christ spoken of in the end times, I wonder how many today are deceived in the same way.

Jesus says to her "I who speak to you am he." Finally, she

understands and believes, and she goes to town to tell everyone she knows about this man, this prophet, this Messiah, this Savior, that she has met. Of course, there is another sermon here about testimony and evangelism, but I'll save that one... But, let me just say that because of her testimony, it says that many from the town came to see him, and the story ends with Jesus staying with them for two days and verse 41 says "because of his words many more became believers". And, they finally get the total revelation of who Jesus is as they say at the end of verse 42 – "we know that this man really is the Savior of the world".

A dear elderly lady was teaching a Sunday School class, and one day the lesson was about building the temple of God. The teacher explained that when the temple was finished, "the pres-ence of the Lord filled the temple". Instantly the eyes of all the children got wide and full as they imagined that huge building filled with presents from God!

Sometimes we are more like them than we like to think. At times we are more concerned about presents from God rather than being in the presence of God. When we come to worship, it should lead us to a growing revelation of who He is, what He can do, and who we are in His presence; knowing that He wants to know us in a more intimate way. I think we all go through or have gone through this progressive revelation of who Jesus is. For some he may just be a good man who lived long ago – far, far, away – you need to know that he is so much more than that; He may have been a wonderful teacher or prophet, or, you may even know and believe him to be the

Christ, the Messiah sent by God. But, until you come to a total revelation of knowing him as your Savior, you don't really know him at all. I hope you can say that you know him today, and that like the woman at the well, you are willing and even excited about making him known to others.

"Three Stages of Transformation"

God wants a transformation to take place in your life – and this isn't just any ordinary transformation. This is a transformation that is super-natural in nature. Something that cannot, does not, and will not occur naturally.

I found something interesting about this word transform or transformation. The word transform or transformation is found three times in the NIV translation of the New Testament. And, there are actually two different Greek words that have been translated the same way. The first word "metamorphoo" is used in two of the instances and refers to an inner kind of change (one that affects character and moral behavior). Then there is the word "meta-schematizo" which refers to a change in appearance or an outward change. These describe what I want to put before you today; and that is, what I find to be, three different "stages" of transformation. There is a beginning transformation; (that which begins to change us inside; then there is a process of transformation; where that which is changing IN us begins to show up on the outside; and then there is an end or finished product...that which has been transformed.

It starts with Romans 12:1-2...

"Therefore, I urge you, brothers, in view of God's mercy, to offer your bodies as living sacrifices, holy and pleasing to God--this is your spiritual act of worship. Do not conform any longer to the pattern of this world, but be *transformed* by the renewing of your mind. Then you will be able to test and approve what God's will is--his good, pleasing and perfect will."

Supernatural transformation begins with the sacrifice of ourselves to God and the acceptance of his grace through Jesus Christ. It's the transforming power of the Holy Spirit convicting us, causing us to question our stinkin thinkin…and bringing us to a point of decision….that point which we call "born again". That point where the truth of God's Word, the Bible, finally sinks in! You could say that when we are born again the inner transformation – the work of the Holy Spirit IN us has begun.

In one sense this transformation is begun and completed with this initial decision for Christ. The reason why this is true is because God's perspective of what has happened to us is so much different from our perspective of what is happening to us! When God looks at a believer He sees the *transformed* soul or spirit of the believer. He sees the *new self* which has been birthed by the grace of God through the believer's faith in Christ. He sees the completed process already done.

When we look at ourselves we see an incomplete picture because we are still in this world. We may even think to ourselves that nothing has really changed. So while we know that there is something different in our lives – there seems to be a struggle between that something different that we feel in our lives and what has always been there.

What we don't immediately realize is that our spirit – which once was dead because of sin – is now alive through the grace of God; and our lives which once were limited to the natural realm, are now set free by the super-natural contact we can have with God. We not only are able to understand and grow in God's Word, but because we understand God's Word, we begin to understand more about life itself! We begin to see the connection between God's Word and life itself.

It is our spirit that is alive within us with salvation that enables us to sense and know and commune with God...something that was missing...has been transformed...completely and fully in an instant! "It's a mystery" as the Apostle Paul would say. But, here is the problem; because we are still in our earthly bodies that are subject to sin and death – it sometimes takes a while for the supernatural transformation that has happened instantaneously in our spirits to "catch up" or filter on down into our everyday lives. That is why Paul often used the language of "*old self*" and "*new self*" because of the dilemma we have as Christians where we have been given a *new* nature by God that is in conflict within the abiding place of where our *old* nature once resided...and controlled. And, this is why he tells us that it is *our job* to "put off the old self...and put on the new self".

This leads us to the second part...

Ephesians 4:22- "You were taught, with regard to your former way of life, to put off your old self, which is being corrupted by its deceitful desires; to be made new in the attitude of your minds; and to put on the new self, created to be like God in true righteousness and holiness."

"You put off…" You see, we have a part in this transformation process. When Paul writes in Ephesians, "Put on your new self" he is recognizing that we have a new nature that must eventually take the place of the control and effects of the old nature still residing our lives. But remember, the Word says that if you know Jesus Christ as Lord and Savior, we are to "reckon our old nature to be dead" – your sinful nature is DEAD, according to the scriptures. Well, if it is dead, why then is there still a battle? It's because we haven't buried it yet! We haven't done Romans 12:1 in our lives yet…"offer yourselves as living sacrifices." So we struggle with our old nature, with the leftover residue of our old nature still in our lives. That is why there is still the *process* of supernatural transformation taking place in our lives here on earth. A good example of this is 2 Corinthians 3:18 - "And we, who with unveiled faces all reflect the Lord's glory, are ***being transformed*** into his likeness with ever-increasing glory, which comes from the Lord, who is the Spirit."

2 Corinthians is clear that there is a process of transformation that takes place in the life of a believer. And it's this process that God wants every single one of us to go through. It's the process of aligning our physical selves with the new creation now found in our spiritual selves. Unlike the change that takes place in our spirit which is instantaneous – the change that takes place in our heart takes time. And, I say "heart" because it is the center of who we are, what we are, and what we do. You see God not only wants us to be transformed into the likeness of Christ, He wants us to be transparent in order for the world to see the power of Christ in us.

Max Lucado coins a phrase that captures what I believe God's desire is for each of us, "God loves you just the way you are, but he refuses to leave you that way" - so we have the process of being transformed.

So, let me review this again; there is a beginning transformation (that which begins to change us inside.) I would say that this begins in the mind. This is when we make up our mind that God does exist; and that the Bible – His Word is true; that Jesus is who He is and has done what God the Father sent him to do; and we accept his offer of salvation. Then what is in our mind drops to our heart and the first stage of transformation is complete.

Then there is a process of transformation; where that which is changing IN us begins to show up on the outside. It changes how we think; how we speak; how we act and react to life. It does not change how we look; age does that! But in a sense we become a new and different person.

And then there is an end or finished product…that which has been transformed. There is what the Bible describes in Philippians 3:21 as the finished product - "who, by the power that enables him to bring everything under his control, will transform our lowly bodies so that they will be like his glorious body." The Greek word used here is meta-schem-a-tizo which if you will remember refers to a change of form – an outward change. This passage refers to the hope that every Christian can have. That one day, Jesus Christ will finish completely what he began here on earth. "He who began a good work in you will be faithful to complete it." He will transform our bodies (which are subject to sin and death) to be like His glorious body…and the process will be complete.

God gave us a perfect example of all this in nature. A caterpillar looks like a fuzzy, fat worm that crawls along from place to place and eats leaves. All the while it has within itself a beautiful butterfly! It just has not transformed yet! When it enters the cocoon, the transformation process takes place. That which was within comes out, and the change is a butterfly. The butterfly is no longer an ugly, fat, worm…it now can fly and not crawl and it enjoys the sweet nectar of the beautiful flowers that God created for it to enjoy!

Now, let me ask you this; can the transforming process be seen in your life?" I ask because it is a noticeable difference. I have said before that Jesus is like bleach in the laundry, once He comes in, there is going to be a change!

Matthew 13:16-23 – "But blessed are your eyes because they see, and your ears because they hear. For truly I tell you, many prophets and righteous people longed to see what you see but did not see it, and to hear what you hear but did not hear it.

"Listen then to what the parable of the sower means: When anyone hears the message about the kingdom and does not understand it, the evil one comes and snatches away what was sown in their heart. This is the seed sown along the path. The seed falling on rocky ground refers to someone who hears the word and at once receives it with joy. But since they have no root, they last only a short time. When trouble or persecution comes because of the word, they quickly fall away. The seed falling among the thorns refers to someone who hears the word, but the worries of this life and the deceitfulness of wealth choke the word, making it unfruitful. But the seed falling on good soil refers to someone who hears the word and understands it. This is the one who produces a crop, yielding a hundred, sixty or thirty times what was sown."

1 Samuel 3:1-10 – "The boy Samuel ministered before the LORD under Eli. In those days the word of the LORD was rare; there were not many visions. One night Eli, whose eyes were becoming so weak that he could barely see, was lying down in his usual place. The lamp of God had not yet gone out, and Samuel was lying down in the house of the LORD, where the ark of God was. Then the LORD called Samuel.

Samuel answered, "Here I am." And he ran to Eli and said, "Here I am; you called me."

But Eli said, "I did not call; go back and lie down." So he went and lay down.

Again the LORD called, "Samuel!" And Samuel got up and went to Eli and said, "Here I am; you called me."

"My son," Eli said, "I did not call; go back and lie down."

Now Samuel did not yet know the LORD: The word of the LORD had not yet been revealed to him.

A third time the LORD called, "Samuel!" And Samuel got up and went to Eli and said, "Here I am; you called me."

Then Eli realized that the LORD was calling the boy. So Eli told Samuel, "Go and lie down, and if he calls you, say, 'Speak, LORD, for your servant is listening.'" So Samuel went and lay down in his place.
The LORD came and stood there, calling as at the other times, "Samuel! Samuel!"
Then Samuel said, "Speak, for your servant is listening."

Eight times in the gospels and eight times in the Book of Revelation, Jesus used the words "let he who has ears, hear what the Spirit is speaking." Basically, he was saying; "If you have ears, use them!" Physical ears? Yes, but even more so "spiritual ears". In fact, it is not so much our ears that Jesus is concerned about as much as our "developing a listening heart."

There are many ways to interpret and preach the parable of the sower. It's the story of a farmer who scattered seed (which is symbolic of the Word of God) and he scattered it in four different types of ground. Most often we think of the ground or the soil as being the condition of the heart, but for our purposes here, let's think of the soil being our ears!

Some ears are hard ground and are simply unreceptive to the Word of God. I mean, when these ears are in church, all they hear is "Blah, blah, blah, blah...mumbo, jumbo, bamboozle!" It's not that they can't hear, it's just that their soil is hard, everything bounces off...and they don't hear anything they can use.

Some ears are like rocky soil. They have selective hearing. There are only certain things they hear. But, what they do hear, they retain. For instance, you could ask just about anyone - Christian or not –

about Noah and they could tell you he built an ark. Ask about Moses - (He was the first one to break the Ten Commandments. *Joke*.) You could ask about Adam and Eve; Daniel in the lion's den; and all the other well known Bible stories, even the story of the Cross, and they will tell you at least something they know about these because they have heard about them…But, they are just stories which have no root, because the soil is rocky and selective.

Some have weedy ears…(Most of the ladies immediately think about their husbands) What kinds of weeds fill our ears? (TV, News, Gossip, rumors, politics, etc.) There are too many other things that compete for their hearing and listening pleasure, and so the seed of God's Word doesn't have a chance; it gets crowded out by all the weeds.

Then, there are those who have good ears, receptive ears, attentive ears, ears that are always listening for and ready to act upon God's voice. His voice may be heard in the singing, the prayers, the message, or the spoken scripture, but wherever and whenever God speaks, they are receptive. They are like Samuel - "Thy servant is listening"…and they can hear God.

In all four cases, the seed is the same, the sower is the same, what is different is the listeners ear! And, if the ratio of this story is significant, three out of four were not listening or could not hear…That means 75% are missing the message!

How do we develop a listening heart? First of all, the Philips version of Romans 12:12 says; "Base your happiness on your hope in Christ. When trials come, endure them patiently; steadfastly *maintain the habit of prayer*". The habit of prayer! It's not a hobby like something we do in our spare time, but a habit. If you look at all the times Jesus went off to pray in scripture, it was always followed by some dramatic or miraculous event. When we are in the habit of prayer, we will develop a listening heart and a listening ear and something may actually happen in our lives!...Let me take that a step further and say that some things may be prevented from happening in our lives...because we are listening!

James 1:25 says; "The man who looks into the perfect law, the law of liberty, *and makes a habit of doing so*, will hear and not forget!" And, "he will be blessed in what he does"! He is talking about making a habit of spending time in God's Word.

There are many who understand this to be true, but give excuse; and excuses are like skunks, they all stink! "I'm just so busy", "I always get interrupted", "I just can't seem to stay regular in this"...So, rather than spend time with God and develop a listening heart and "good soil" we let others spend time with Him and then think we will benefit from their experience. Isn't that what we pay the pastor to do? Isn't that what our S.S. teachers do? Isn't that why we read books? We want to benefit from someone else's experience with God.

I want to challenge you with this thought; "Do we do that with other parts of our lives?" Like; "Vacations are such a hassle, I'm going to send someone else on vacation for me, I'll pay for it, and then I can hear all about it when they come back"??? I'm in love with that person, but I'm so busy, I'll let someone else romance her, then he can tell me what it's like, and someday I'll marry her"??? Or, how about; "Chewing is so much trouble, I'll let someone else chew my food, and then I'll just swallow whatever he gives me"??? That's just gross! If we would never do that for anything else, why would we do it with God? God wants to speak to us first-hand! And, He wants us to develop a listening ear.

These two habits of prayer and bible reading go hand in hand. We need to pray for understanding and enlightenment before we read and after we read. The Bible is not a newspaper to be skimmed through, it is a mine that contains precious gold and silver that needs to be quarried out. Proverbs 2:4 says that insight and understanding and wisdom will come if "you search for it like silver and hunt for it like hidden treasure"..."Then you will understand the fear of the Lord and find the knowledge of God."

If you want to know someone who developed a listening ear and heart for God, just read about the rest of Samuel's life. This is a lot to think about, but I want you to take this thought with you today; "A listening heart is something that needs to be developed." It is soil that needs to cultivated. It is something we must do firsthand!

Exodus 13:20 - 14:28 – "After leaving Sukkoth they camped at Etham on the edge of the desert. By day the LORD went ahead of them in a pillar of cloud to guide them on their way and by night in a pillar of fire to give them light, so that they could travel by day or night. Neither the pillar of cloud by day nor the pillar of fire by night left its place in front of the people.

Then the LORD said to Moses, "Tell the Israelites to turn back and encamp near Pi Hahiroth, between Migdol and the sea. They are to encamp by the sea, directly opposite Baal Zephon. Pharaoh will think, 'The Israelites are wandering around the land in confusion, hemmed in by the desert.' And I will harden Pharaoh's heart, and he will pursue them. But I will gain glory for myself through Pharaoh and all his army, and the Egyptians will know that I am the LORD." So the Israelites did this.

When the king of Egypt was told that the people had fled, Pharaoh and his officials changed their minds about them and said, "What have we done? We have let the Israelites go and have lost their services!" So he had his chariot made ready and took his army with him. He took six hundred of the best chariots, along with all the other chariots of Egypt, with officers over all of them. The LORD hardened the heart of Pharaoh king of Egypt, so that he pursued the Israelites, who were marching out boldly. The Egyptians—all Pharaoh's horses and chariots, horsemen and troops—pursued the Israelites and overtook them as they camped by the sea near Pi Hahiroth, opposite Baal Zephon.

As Pharaoh approached, the Israelites looked up, and there were the Egyptians, marching after them. They were terrified and cried out to the LORD. They said to Moses, "Was it because there were no graves in Egypt that you brought us to the desert to die? What have you done to us by bringing us out of Egypt? Didn't we say to you in Egypt, 'Leave us alone; let us serve the Egyptians'? It would have been better for us to serve the Egyptians than to die in the desert!"

Moses answered the people, "Do not be afraid. Stand firm and you will see the deliverance the LORD will bring you today. The Egyptians you see today you will never see again. The LORD will fight for you; you need only to be still." Then the LORD said to

Moses, "Why are you crying out to me? Tell the Israelites to move on.

Raise your staff and stretch out your hand over the sea to divide the water so that the Israelites can go through the sea on dry ground. I will harden the hearts of the Egyptians so that they will go in after them. And I will gain glory through Pharaoh and all his army, through his chariots and his horsemen. The Egyptians will know that I am the LORD when I gain glory through Pharaoh, his chariots and his horsemen."

Then the angel of God, who had been traveling in front of Israel's army, withdrew and went behind them. The pillar of cloud also moved from in front and stood behind them, coming between the armies of Egypt and Israel. Throughout the night the cloud brought darkness to the one side and light to the other side; so neither went near the other all night long.

Then Moses stretched out his hand over the sea, and all that night the LORD drove the sea back with a strong east wind and turned it into dry land. The waters were divided, and the Israelites went through the sea on dry ground, with a wall of water on their right and on their left.

The Egyptians pursued them, and all Pharaoh's horses and chariots and horsemen followed them into the sea. During the last watch of the night the LORD looked down from the pillar of fire and cloud at the Egyptian army and threw it into confusion. He jammed the wheels of their chariots so that they had difficulty driving. And the Egyptians said, "Let's get away from the Israelites! The LORD is fighting for them against Egypt."

Then the LORD said to Moses, "Stretch out your hand over the sea so that the waters may flow back over the Egyptians and their chariots and horsemen." Moses stretched out his hand over the sea, and at daybreak the sea went back to its place. The Egyptians were fleeing toward it, and the LORD swept them into the sea. The water flowed back and covered the chariots and horsemen—the entire army of Pharaoh that had followed the Israelites into the sea. Not one of them survived."

1 Corinthians 1:19-25 – "For it is written: "I will destroy the wisdom of the wise; the intelligence of the intelligent I will frustrate." Where is the wise person? Where is the teacher of the law? Where is the philosopher of this age? Has not God made foolish the wisdom of

the world? For since in the wisdom of God the world through its wisdom did not know him, God was pleased through the foolishness of what was preached to save those who believe. Jews demand signs and Greeks look for wisdom, but we preach Christ crucified: a stumbling block to Jews and foolishness to Gentiles, but to those whom God has called, both Jews and Greeks, Christ the power of God and the wisdom of God. For the foolishness of God is wiser than human wisdom, and the weakness of God is stronger than human strength."

One of the most dramatic scenes in the movie "The Ten Commandments" starring Charlton Heston, is Moses parting the Red Sea. The Israelites were starting a new chapter in their lives after over 400 years of captivity in Egypt. To gain perspective on that, we would have to go back to 1606 some five generations ago, and say our great, great, great, great, grandparents went into captivity and we are just now - five generations later being called out! While there were many who grew up in Egypt not knowing the Lord, there were also many who kept the faith alive and taught their children and their grandchildren all about God and His promise of one day sending a Savior to set the captives free.

Well, the Israelites left Egypt under the leadership of Moses, and had marched to the Red Sea as they were told. Now they find themselves with the Sea blocking their way to freedom, and as if to make a bad situation worse, they have the Egyptians in hot pursuit! They were literally between the devil and the deep blue sea.

What happened in this crucial time of Israel's journey reveals some truths I believe come shinning through and are applicable to us today. We to are on a journey; through time and space we wander through this life headed for eternity; headed for the promised land. Quite often we also find ourselves in situations where something seems to be blocking our progress forward, and we have the enemy Satan hot on our trail pursuing us from our past. We look into the unknown future, and we just don't know what lies ahead, and our past seems to pursue us no matter how hard we try to forget... and we have a choice to make. I want to show you three things from this scripture story:

#1. We need to realize that God goes before us to prepare the way, to prepare the future, and to guide us into the future.

#2. We need to know that God is also our rear guard, who can separate us from and take care of our past.

#3. We must understand that many experiences in life have a double meaning, depending on which side of the cloud you are on!

First, let's look at God leading us into the future. We must begin with the realization that God is Sovereign over all things. He is who He says He is, and He can do what He says he can do! Isaiah 40:22 says: "He sits enthroned above the circle of the earth, He stretches out the heavens like a canopy, He brings princes to naught and reduces the rulers of this world to nothing"...and verse 28 goes on "The Lord is the everlasting God, the creator of the ends of the earth. He will not grow tired or weary"...And finally, verse 31 - which we are all familiar with - "but, those who hope in the Lord" – Now hope is a future word, So, those who put their future and their faith in God, who holds their future in his hands – "they will renew their strength. They will soar on wings like eagles; they will run and not grow weary; they will walk and not faint."

Notice the future tense of the words; "they *will* run, they *will* walk, they *will* soar"! Not when we depend on the economy; not when we depend on knowledge or technology; not when we depend on what we have or don't have; not when we look to the future in our own strength and ability; but, when we wait upon the Lord and trust the future into the one who holds the future!

As the Israelites stood on the banks of the Red Sea, they saw a barrier in the way of their future. But, Moses said in verse 13 - "Do not be afraid. Stand firm and you will see the deliverance the Lord will bring you today!" Vs 16 - "Then the Lord said to Moses - Tell the Israelites to move on. Stretch your hand over the sea to divide the water, so the Israelites can go through on dry ground!" They saw a barrier to the future, but God knew they wouldn't even get their feet wet!

Secondly, look at verse 19 - "Then the angel of God, who had been traveling in front of Israel's army…withdrew and went behind them." The pillar of cloud also moved from in front and moved behind them, coming between the armies of Egypt and Israel. God not only holds the future and goes before us; but God is also our rear guard; He guards our past! The Israelites saw their past pursuing them, and that's when the panic began.

We may think we have escaped the ghost of our past, when suddenly we hear the clatter of horses hooves and the dust of chariot wheels! Some of us are pursued by fears, inhibitions, frustrations and phobias that psychologists tell us are the fruit of seeds sown in childhood experiences. Past abuse, past fears, past whatever it may be, a heavy burden or grief, some old sin or temptation, the truth is that the Israelites had left Egypt, but Egypt had not left the Israelites!

For many of us, we may think we are no longer part of the world, but the truth is that the world is still part of us! Worldly thinking, worldly feelings and actions we can't seem to shake. You can be sure that the enemy will always pursue us with our past, but we can stand firm in the faith that God has taken care of our past. Our past has been forgiven and forgotten. God is our rear guard as well as the one who goes before us preparing the future.

Finally, look at the last part of verse 20 - "Throughout the night the cloud brought darkness to the one side and light to the other!" So, you see, our perspective of the future, and our perspective of the past, depends on which side of the cloud we are on! The Egyptians saw only darkness. The Israelites only light. The same fire that melts wax hardens clay. With faith our experiences in life mean one thing; without faith, they mean another. "The things of the Spirit are foolishness to those who are without the Spirit." The old saying; "to see the light" means that we have come out from the dark side of the cloud and are walking in the light of God's Word. We are seeing things in a different light, from a different perspective.

Consider the Cross: 1st Corinthians 1:23 says that "Unto the Jews the Cross is a stumbling block, and to the Greek, foolishness, but unto us who are saved it is the power of God!" As we march toward the future, let's keep in step with the Spirit of God, putting our faith and trust in God, who goes before us to prepare our future! And, let's put the past behind us, and strain ahead, knowing that God is our rear guard! He's got the past covered! Let's stay on the light side…and continue to walk in the light as He is in the light!

1st Thessalonians 5:1-11 –"Now, brothers and sisters, about times and dates we do not need to write to you, for you know very well that the day of the Lord will come like a thief in the night. While people are saying, "Peace and safety," destruction will come on them suddenly, as labor pains on a pregnant woman, and they will not escape.

But you, brothers and sisters, are not in darkness so that this day should surprise you like a thief. You are all children of the light and children of the day. We do not belong to the night or to the darkness. So then, let us not be like others, who are asleep, but let us be awake and sober. For those who sleep, sleep at night, and those who get drunk, get drunk at night. But since we belong to the day, let us be sober, putting on faith and love as a breastplate, and the hope of salvation as a helmet. For God did not appoint us to suffer wrath but to receive salvation through our Lord Jesus Christ. He died for us so that, whether we are awake or asleep, we may live together with him. Therefore encourage one another and build each other up, just as in fact you are doing."

1st Thessalonians 1:2-8a –"We always thank God for all of you and continually mention you in our prayers. We remember before our God and Father your work produced by faith, your labor prompted by love, and your endurance inspired by hope in our Lord Jesus Christ.

For we know, brothers and sisters loved by God, that he has chosen you, because our gospel came to you not simply with words but also with power, with the Holy Spirit and deep conviction. You know how we lived among you for your sake. You became imitators of us and of the Lord, for you welcomed the message in the midst of severe suffering with the joy given by the Holy Spirit. And so you became a model to all the believers in Macedonia and Achaia. The Lord's message rang out from you not only in Macedonia and Achaia—your faith in God has become known everywhere."

As a youngster, I was involved in a 4-H club. I remember the 4 H's were - "Head, Heart, Hands, and Health". The 4-H clubs were a big part of the County Fair every year, and there were several categories you could be involved in. Mine were leather-craft and woodworking. The goal and the reward for your displays of course, were blue, red, or yellow ribbons identifying 1st, 2nd, or 3rd place. In all my years of involvement no one that I know of tried their best to get third place!

In 1st Corinthians 9:24, Paul says that we all ought to "run as if to win the prize". I want to give you four things that will help us as Christians, to win the prize; to receive the crown of righteousness! Think of this as being a "4-H" Christian, only the four "H's" are: Hopefulness, Helpfulness, Happiness, and Holiness.

One day while hunting, Larry and Elmer got lost in the woods. Trying to reassure his friend, Larry said "Don't worry, all we have to do is shoot in the air three times (which is the universal hunting code for "I'm lost and need help") stay where we are, and someone will come and find us." So they shot in the air three times and waited… but no one came. After a while they shot three times again…still no one came. Feeling hopeless, they decided to try once more, Elmer said "I sure hope it works this time, we're down to our last three arrows!" (I just wanted to loosen you up a little!)

The first thing we need in order to win in this Christian life is "Hopefulness". The hopefulness of a Christian is based on Paul's teaching in the chapter previous to our text, chapter four verses 13-18…"Brothers, we do not want you to be ignorant about those who fall asleep, or to grieve like the rest of men, who have no hope. We believe that Jesus died and rose again and so we believe that God will bring with Jesus those who have fallen asleep in him. According to the Lord's own word, we tell you that we who are still alive, who are left till the coming of the Lord, will certainly not precede those who have fallen asleep. For the Lord himself will come down from heaven, with a loud command, with the voice of the archangel and with the trumpet call of God, and the dead in Christ will rise first. After that, we who are still alive and are left will be caught up together with them in the clouds to meet the Lord in the air. And so we will be with the Lord forever. Therefore encourage each other with these words." Put this together with 5:9-10 of our text - "For God did not appoint us to suffer wrath but to receive salvation through our Lord Jesus Christ. He died for us so that, whether we are awake or asleep, we may live together with him. Therefore encourage one another and build each other up, just as in fact you are doing."...This is our hope!

Hope is vital - in fact it's critical for our every day survival in life. God understands that. That's why in Romans 15:4 we are told: "For everything that was written in the past was written to teach us, so that through endurance and the encouragement of the Scriptures we might have HOPE." When we speak of this type of hope it could best be described as an attitude of confidence, expectation, and trust; no matter what the circumstance.

While "hope" is a future word, the hope of Christ's return and our rapture, and the eternal rewards of heaven, are not just something we "hope" will come in the future someday…in the sweet by and by; this is our present hope! It also is not just "wishful thinking". It is absolute belief, absolute trust, absolute assurance, that God will do what He says He will do! We are not called to hope that it might, maybe, possibly will happen, but that Christ IS coming and it could be at any given moment of time! In the twinkling of an eye the Word says!

Our hope is based on fact! By the way, Robert Schuller II said something that bears repeating and quoting in every church around the world today; He was speaking to the issue of the Davinci Code, and to the fact that it is pure fiction and is found in the fiction section of the book store…And he said, "The book that I believe in, the book that I base my life and my future upon is not fiction!" Where is your hope today? Is it based on absolute fact, or just wishful thinking? In order to have any hope for the future, we must have a relationship with the one who holds the future.

Of course, the hopefulness of a Christian is more than a hope of heaven, it holds out hope for all things. Our relationship with God gives us a hope for a better future for our families; a better future for our extended church family; a better future for our world; not because we think life is just a bed of roses, but because we know that no matter what we may face in the future, God is on our side and He is by our side! "He works all things out for the good of those who love him." (Romans 8:28) "If God is for us, who can be against us?" "He who did not spare his own Son, but gave him up for us all—how will he not also, along with him, graciously give us all things? Who will bring any charge against those whom God has chosen? It is God who justifies. Who is he that condemns? Christ Jesus, who died—more than that, who was raised to life—is at the right hand of God and is also interceding for us. Who shall separate us from the love of Christ? Shall trouble or hardship or persecution or famine or nakedness or danger or sword? No, in all these things we are more than conquerors through him who loved us. For I am convinced that neither death nor life, neither angels nor demons, neither the present nor the future, nor any powers, neither height nor depth, nor anything else in all creation, will be able to separate us from the love of God that is in Christ Jesus our Lord." (Romans 8:31-39)

My friends, that is a positive HOPE! It is a hope that the world does not have. All who are in Christ are "blue ribbon" - #number 1 - first place Christians because of our hopefulness!

Some Christians seem to be hopeful and doubtful at the same time. A Christian cannot be hopeful and worry about the future at the same time. There is a way to overcome worry and doubt; the Apostle Paul tells us how in Philippians 4:8 - Before we go there let me tell you a story about my Grandfather's coffee; Gramps had the old time percolating pots that you put on the stove. Instead of taking the time to clean out the coffee grounds and the pot, he would just add water and more grounds! Thank God for coffee filters! And, water filters; and furnace filters; and pool filters; gas filters, oil filters and air filters…What does a filter do? It filters out the bad, the unwanted, the evil, and allows the good to flow through! In Philippians 4:8 Paul tells us we need to filter our minds in order to remain hopeful; He says; "Whatever is true, whatever is noble, whatever is right, pure, lovely, admirable, if anything is excellent or praiseworthy - think about such things." Why? Because negative thoughts bring us down and they destroy our hope! It is easier to filter out the bad and fill up with the good than it is to try and remove the bad later.

When it comes to "running as if to win the prize" Hebrews 10:23 says "Let us hold unswervingly to the hope we profess, for He who promised is faithful." Hopeful, Helpful, Happy and Holy Christians are always winners!

Ephesians 4:29-5:2 – "Do not let any unwholesome talk come out of your mouths, but only what is helpful for building others up according to their needs, that it may benefit those who listen. And do not grieve the Holy Spirit of God, with whom you were sealed for the day of redemption. Get rid of all bitterness, rage and anger, brawling and slander, along with every form of malice. Be kind and compassionate to one another, forgiving each other, just as in Christ God forgave you. Follow God's example, therefore, as dearly loved children and walk in the way of love, just as Christ loved us and gave himself up for us as a fragrant offering and sacrifice to God."

2 Corinthians 1:3-4 – "Praise be to the God and Father of our Lord Jesus Christ, the Father of compassion and the God of all comfort, who comforts us in all our troubles, so that we can comfort those in any trouble with the comfort we ourselves receive from God."

Romans 12:9-16 – "Love must be sincere. Hate what is evil; cling to what is good. Be devoted to one another in love. Honor one another above yourselves. Never be lacking in zeal, but keep your spiritual fervor, serving the Lord. Be joyful in hope, patient in affliction, faithful in prayer. Share with the Lord's people who are in need. Practice hospitality.
 Bless those who persecute you; bless and do not curse. Rejoice with those who rejoice; mourn with those who mourn. Live in harmony with one another. Do not be proud, but be willing to associate with people of low position. Do not be conceited.

We are looking at four things that are characteristic of - as well as God's expectations of Christians: "Hopefulness", which is a look forward; "Helpfulness" which is a look outward; "Happiness" which is a look inward; and Holiness" which is a look upward!

We looked at "Hopefulness" - There are far too many people

living in this world who have no hope! Paul says in 1ˢᵗ Thessalonians 4:13 - "Brothers, we do not want you to be ignorant about those who have died, or to grieve like the rest of men who have no hope." How horrible to live life thinking that this is all there is…that death is the end of life! A Christian is an ever hopeful person.

Next, I want to look at the "Helpfulness" of the Christian, which is an outward look. As it concerns the helpfulness of a Christian, I invite you to look with me to the continuation of our scripture from yesterday; 1ˢᵗ Thessalonians 5:12…"Now we ask you, brothers, to respect those who work hard among you, who are over you in the Lord and who admonish you. Hold them in the highest regard in love because of their work. Live in peace with each other. And we urge you, brothers, warn those who are idle, encourage the timid, help the weak, be patient with everyone. Make sure that nobody pays back wrong for wrong, but always try to be kind to each other and to everyone else." This is the "helpful" mark of the Christian.

A couple of years ago, I did a sermon in which I spoke about "Observations from the chicken pen". It had to do with the fact that chickens are always chasing one another around; they are always picking on and pecking at one another; and when one of them has a problem or a sore of some sort, rather than being helpful, they will pick and pick until the one with the problem practically bleeds to death! …But then, we're not like chickens… are we?

I realize that a lot of hurts go undetected, but the church is supposed to be a safe place where we can share our hurts with friends. Some of us do not know how to respond to hurts. Our scripture told us to: "mourn with those who mourn" or "weep with them that weep" and "rejoice with those who rejoice." Now these commands were written NOT to the elders or to church leaders, but to all Christians. God demands that we all are helpful to each other. So let me ask you this question: How good are you at comforting others? How good are you at weeping with those who weep? Some of you are probably skilled in these areas; too many of us are absolutely awful in this department, while many would say they are probably somewhere in between.

Today I am going to try to be "helpful" by "helping" us all in the area of being "helpful" rather than hurting. This is an important skill to learn, for you will use it in every relationship you have.

#1. The Most Important Piece of Advice: Shut Up and Listen. Sometimes this is the most helpful thing we can do. I have to admit this is a hard one from me because I am usually quick to offer advise, when there are many times it would be better for me to be quiet and just listen. In the Book of Job, Job's friends were wonderful--until they opened their mouths and tried to fix things; they told stories of their experiences and thought they had everything figured out, just what was really wrong and what Job ought to do...and boy, were they wrong!

In chapter 2 11-13 it says that Job's friends "Eliphaz, Bildad and Zophar, heard about all the troubles that had come upon him, they set out from their homes and met together by agreement to go and sympathize with him and comfort him. "When they saw him from a distance, they could hardly recognize him; they began to weep aloud, and they tore their robes and sprinkled dust on their heads. Then they sat on the ground with him for seven days and seven nights. No one said a word to him, because they saw how great his suffering was." If they would have left it at that they would have been fine. We ought to remember that comforters are welcome; but <u>counselors should come by invitation only.</u> If you really want to help others during times of crisis, grief, tragedy, personal loss, or even depression, it helps to know what you are doing... Are you there to listen and help, or to be a counselor?

#2. Do not minimize their problems in any way. Proverbs 25:20 reads: "Like one who takes away a garment on a cold day, or like vinegar poured on soda, is one who sings songs to a heavy heart." This simply means we have tried to minimize the problem; "Oh, it's not all that bad." "Come on now, don't worry, be happy!" I have a bad habit of doing this. I hate to see people sad or depressed, so I try to get them to smile or joke around in some way. While in my mind I may be trying to help, I am in reality minimizing their problem! Jeremiah 6:14, says "They dress the wound of my people as though it were not serious. `Peace, peace,' they say, when there is no peace."

Here is another example: a person says: "It is so depressing being out of work so long, I just don't know what to do; this has really got me down." (Right Response): "I don't blame you for feeling the way you do. It is a bad situation, and I would probably have some of those same thoughts as well. I want to pray with you about this. Let's talk about it so I will better know how to pray." (Here is a Dumb Response): "What are you so down about. Don't you realize it could be much worse! Take my friend Joe for instance, he got laid off and now he has lung cancer!" (Here's an even Dumber Response): Well, the Bible tells us to "rejoice in the Lord"…Set your eyes on Him" and don't fret about being out of work…God will work it out! (Here is the Dumbest Response): You are just not trusting God! He must have brought these troubles upon you to punish you, discipline you, or teach you something." This leads to number three.

#3. Do not condemn or put them down in any way. Express that it is okay for a Christian to feel afraid, worry, or be angry...and even doubt. These are natural, human, responses. All of these things beset Moses, King David, the Prophet Habbakkuk, and there will be times when we will feel these as well… Mature Christians understand that we can feel fear, worry, grief, and even anger, and still have faith and hope! It is even worse to deny any of these feelings. Remember, according to our scripture, the things we go through are meant to train us to empathize and help others...

Finally, even if people bring troubles upon themselves, remember, they are still hurting. It never helps to say things like; "You made your bed, now sleep in it" or "You reap what you sow!" These are not proper responses at the time! We should not add to the consequences of their experience with a guilt trip! Jesus did not come to rub sin in, but to rub it out. The Holy Spirit is called the "Comforter"…The "Helper"…Our "guide"…He is our "help" in time of need! Those who practice "helpfulness" are winners as Christians.

Paul, the apostle, once said, "When I was a child, I talked like a child, I thought like a child, I reasoned like a child. When I became a man, I put childish ways behind me." (1 Corinthians 13:11) I think it's time we live life to our full potential by realizing that we who are in Christ, are no longer little kids! Let's stop acting like little kids, and start acting and doing what mature adults are supposed to do! Let's stop being selfish or smug and start being helpful!

I Thessalonians 5:16-18 – "Rejoice always, pray continually, give thanks in all circumstances; for this is God's will for you in Christ Jesus."

Psalm 119:97-112 – "Oh, how I love your law! I meditate on it all day long. Your commands are always with me and make me wiser than my enemies. I have more insight than all my teachers, for I meditate on your statutes. I have more understanding than the elders, for I obey your precepts. I have kept my feet from every evil path so that I might obey your word. I have not departed from your laws, for you yourself have taught me. How sweet are your words to my taste, sweeter than honey to my mouth! I gain understanding from your precepts; therefore I hate every wrong path. Your word is a lamp for my feet, a light on my path. I have taken an oath and confirmed it, that I will follow your righteous laws. I have suffered much; preserve my life, LORD, according to your word. Accept, LORD, the willing praise of my mouth, and teach me your laws. Though I constantly take my life in my hands, I will not forget your law. The wicked have set a snare for me, but I have not strayed from your precepts. Your statutes are my heritage forever; they are the joy of my heart. My heart is set on keeping your decrees to the very end.

There are four characteristics that we must have in our lives in order to "run the race" as the Apostle Paul puts it; or to live the life; or walk the walk; or persistently and patiently, and perpetually carry on in the abundant life that God has chosen for us to have. You see, we can never do that; we will always fall and fail, if we are not consistently hopeful; if we are not consistently and constantly helpful or showing love toward one another. And, we certainly cannot begin to have the motivation to live this life according to

God's Word, if we are not happy. However, our faith and our hope and our love and our motivation in life have as their source the "holiness" or righteousness that God expects and demands.

So, let's talk about happiness. Proverbs 15:13 says "A happy heart makes the face cheerful."

When it comes to happiness, I think everyone would agree that there are basically four things that control the extent of our happiness; And, probably in this order of priority;

#1 Family (This may include all relationships…)

#2 Health

#3 Finances; and,

#4 Possessions.

I think it would be unrealistic to expect that as Christians we ought to always be happy and joyful because the extent of our happiness is affected by these things. However, as I said, happiness is a look inward. There is a reason for that…It's because while the external circumstances of these things may temporarily affect what is going on around us, as Christians we know that true happiness depends on what is happening within us! It is all about having peace IN all circumstances; and giving thanks IN all circumstances; and praying through all circumstances; not FOR or BECAUSE OF. We cannot pretend to be joyful when we are hurting in some way, but we can find strength, and comfort, and trust, and peace in knowing that God is ultimately in control…and that is our inner joy…our inner happiness.

If our faith and trust and even belief in God were to depend on external happiness, most of us would never be happy, and we certainly would not be Christians. "The God of the mountain is still God in the valley!

Psychologists tell us that people need three things to make them happy; they need something to do; they need something to love; and they need something to look forward to. I think scripture would agree with that. However, to be truly happy, we must be doing the right thing, loving the right way, and looking forward to the right thing! True happiness has to do with having the right focus. As Christians we are called to focus on eternity and eternal things. We are to set our minds and our hearts on things above!...Colossians 3:1-3 says "Since, then, you have been raised with Christ, set your hearts on things above, where Christ is seated at the right hand of God. Set your minds on things above, not on earthly things. For you died, and your life is now hidden with Christ in God."

We are to focus on people not possessions. Why? Because people are the only thing of this world that are eternal! We are to focus on service not self. Philippians 2:3-4 "Do nothing out of selfish ambition or vain conceit, but in humility consider others better than yourselves. Each of you should look not only to your own interests, but also to the interests of others." God knows that it brings us joy and we feel blessed when we are helping someone else; that's the way he created us. And, when we are helping others instead of serving self, we are storing up "treasures in heaven". It's all about what's going on within us and not around us.

There once was a very wealthy and successful man. He had more money than he could ever spend and he was admired and looked up to by his community. Still, he knew that something was missing in his life. He wasn't happy. All his life he had pursued happiness and strived for happiness but had never been able to find it. Then one day he heard about a hidden temple in Nepal that had a special room that contained the secret to happiness. He immediately sold all that he owned and set out to find this hidden temple. After many years of searching and countless hardships he arrived there. He was weary and penniless, but he knew that none of that mattered now that he had found the temple. He asked a wise, smiling monk if he could enter the special room. The monk agreed and showed him the stairs leading to the room. He climbed them with legs shaking with anticipation and slowly opened the door. He stared into the room with sun-light streaming through the window and saw what he had come so far to find. There hanging on the wall was the secret of happiness. The man gazed at his reflection in the mirror and laughed.

It is time that we all realized that *we* are the secret to our own happiness. Happiness is a choice that we make within. God loves us and gives each one of us the ability to fill our lives with love, joy, peace, happiness, and oneness with Him. We need only choose to do so day by day. Don't spend your life searching the world for happiness. Just look in the mirror and choose to be happy. Then what's in your heart, will reflect on your face.

Colossians 3:1-17 – "Since, then, you have been raised with Christ, set your hearts on things above, where Christ is, seated at the right hand of God. Set your minds on things above, not on earthly things. For you died, and your life is now hidden with Christ in God. When Christ, who is your life, appears, then you also will appear with him in glory.

Put to death, therefore, whatever belongs to your earthly nature: sexual immorality, impurity, lust, evil desires and greed, which is idolatry. Because of these, the wrath of God is coming. You used to walk in these ways, in the life you once lived. But now you must also rid yourselves of all such things as these: anger, rage, malice, slander, and filthy language from your lips. Do not lie to each other, since you have taken off your old self with its practices and have put on the new self, which is being renewed in knowledge in the image of its Creator. Here there is no Gentile or Jew, circumcised or uncircumcised, barbarian, Scythian, slave or free, but Christ is all, and is in all.

Therefore, as God's chosen people, holy and dearly loved, clothe yourselves with compassion, kindness, humility, gentleness and patience. Bear with each other and forgive one another if any of you has a grievance against someone. Forgive as the Lord forgave you. And over all these virtues put on love, which binds them all together in perfect unity.

Let the peace of Christ rule in your hearts, since as members of one body you were called to peace. And be thankful. Let the message of Christ dwell among you richly as you teach and admonish one another with all wisdom through psalms, hymns, and songs from the Spirit, singing to God with gratitude in your hearts. And whatever you do, whether in word or deed, do it all in the name of the Lord Jesus, giving thanks to God the Father through him.

Romans 6:19-23 – "I am using an example from everyday life because of your human limitations. Just as you used to offer yourselves as slaves to impurity and to ever-increasing wickedness, so now offer yourselves as slaves to righteousness leading to holiness. When you were slaves to sin, you were free from the control of righteousness. What benefit did you reap at that time from the things you are now ashamed of? Those things result in death! But now that you have been set free from sin and have become slaves of God, the benefit you reap leads to holiness, and the result is eternal life. For the wages of sin is death, but the gift of God is eternal life in Christ Jesus our Lord."

---

2 Corinthians 7:1 – "Therefore, since we have these promises, dear friends, let us purify ourselves from everything that contaminates body and spirit, perfecting holiness out of reverence for God."

Hebrews 12:14 – "Make every effort to live in peace with everyone and to be holy; without holiness no one will see the Lord.

We are wrapping up this series that I have titled "Becoming A 4-H Christian" - which is a look at the four things that are the "stand out" attributes or characteristics of a Christian. Not our idea of a Christian...but God's. They are: "Hopefulness, Helpfulness, Happiness, and Holiness." Hopefulness is a look forward. Hopefulness allows us to not only look with assurance and anticipation to the future glory of Christ's coming, and the Rapture, and the wedding supper of the Lamb and the Judgment of rewards, and the eternal reward of heaven...But, also the hope of a better today. A better life, a better family, a better tomorrow, all because of our relationship with God and His Word...But, there's more:

The second "H" was "Helpfulness"... Helpfulness is a look

around. It is the characteristic of a Christian to always be looking for and listening for ways in which we can obey the Command of Christ to "love one another". This is an attribute that real Christians have. Always looking to build up rather than tearing down. Always looking to help and not hinder spiritual growth in another. Always willing to come along side and carry another's burden and help them through a tough time. Real Christians are part of the building crew, not the wrecking crew!

The third "H" we looked at was "Happiness" Proverbs 15:13 - "A happy heart makes the face cheerful". Happiness is a look inward. If the heart is happy, the face will show it. If our faith and trust in God were based on external happiness, most of us would not be happy or Christian. Our happiness, our joy, our peace, comes from what is happening IN us. We cannot pretend to be happy when we are not. We can't pre-tend to be joyful when we are hurting. But God's Word tells us that we can find happiness and joy IN all circumstances, not because of or in spite of, but IN…because we know the one who is in control of all things, and the God of the mountain is still God in the valley, and He will see us through - and even provide a way out. Happiness remember, is a choice. Don't spend your life searching for the world's happiness, just look in the mirror and make the choice to be happy…then what's in your heart will reflect on your face.

Finally, here we are at the fourth "H" - "Holiness". In my N.I.V. Bible, the heading for our text says "Rules For Holy Living." In my Life Application Bible, it says "Principles for Christian Living."

There really is no difference in the context of these headings, but there is a difference in our perception of them. Whether it's in the Bible or somewhere else, it is easier for us to accept the word "principles" but harder to accept "rules". It is easier for us to accept "How to be a Christian" than it is to accept "How to be holy".

The perception seems to be that of desiring, or trying to lead a Christian life by attempting at least, to follow some of the "principles" put forth in God's Word. However, when we talk about "Holy living" we tend to see it as something unattainable and therefore hardly worth trying. That comes from the fact that somehow we equate holiness with absolute perfection. As far as I know, there are only three who are absolutely holy and perfect; the Father, the Son, and the Holy Spirit!

In the Bible it speaks of God as being holy; it talks about Jesus being the holy Son of God; and it talks about the work of the Holy Spirit. But, it also talks about holy mountains, holy temples, holy sacrifices, holy cities, and Israel as God's holy people. None of these were perfect and holy within themselves, they were holy because God's presence made them holy. They were people, places, and things that were set apart for God.

The theme that is interwoven throughout the New Testament is that "in Christ", "through Christ", and "because of Christ", we are holy in God's sight. We are set apart for God. We are crucified, justified, and sanctified by God through Christ. Don't take my word for it, believe God's Word for it! So, in God's eyes - if we are really Christians - we are holy in his sight.

I wish I could say "Well, that's it…You are holy…you can go home now" but, then we have verses like - "<u>Be</u> holy, for I am holy." In other words, because you *are* holy…*be* holy! Or, "Just as you used to do offer the parts of your body" (Which parts? Hands, feet, heart, eyes, brain, voice) "in slavery to impurity and sin, so now offer them in slavery to righteousness - <u>leading to</u> holiness!"…"the benefit you reap <u>leads to</u> holiness, and the result is eternal life".

What about 2 Cor. 7:1 "let us purify ourselves from everything that contaminates body and spirit, <u>perfecting</u> holiness out of reverence for God"? Hebrews 12:14 - "Make every effort to live in peace with all men and <u>to be</u> holy"? What about all the "Rules For Holy Living" given to us in our text? It obviously is a call by God to us saying "Because you are holy, because I have made you holy, you must offer yourselves, and do what it takes to seek after, and perfect those things that lead to the holy and righteous life I expect of you!" And, in case you don't know what they are, here is a partial list of about 20 things you can do – I'll write them down in Collosians chapter three!" Holiness is not just something to have, holiness is something we must live!

Someone once said - "Godly talk does not always imply a Godly walk"! "Painting the pump white does not purify the water"! God expects every Christian to live a holy life, but the idea of exactly how to be holy has suffered from many false concepts. In fact, they almost always lead to legalism. Holiness is equated with a series of prohibitions; "You should not, you must not, you cannot." If we follow this approach we may be in danger of becoming like the

Pharisees with their endless list of rules and regulations and religious "self-righteous" attitude. To some holiness brings images of "bunned" hair, long skirts, black stockings, no make-up, no jewelry, and several other mannerisms. You know what I'm talking about. Holiness is some kind of mold that we must fit into in order to fit as well into the mold we have created for a Christian! It is unattainable perfection, don't even try. God knows the thoughts of your mind, and the emotions and attitudes of your heart, and while you may look holy, God's wondering if you are ever going to DO anything holy!

While we keep concerning ourselves with "how"...God is more concerned with "when". The true, biblical, concept of holiness involves only three things; to be morally blameless; to be separated from sin; and to be fully consecrated to God.

Scripture John 10:10 – "The thief comes only to steal and kill and destroy; I have come that they may have life, and have it to the full."

Our world is full of unhappy and dissatisfied people. For this reason, people everywhere are looking for answers to the emptiness they feel inside. These people will try anything, if it might bring them some sort of satisfaction or happiness. So, what is the solution? Materialism and wealth? I think we have all heard the saying "Money can't buy happiness"... Pleasure and enjoyment? Well they may bring a momentary or temporary sense of happiness or satisfaction...but, soon we know that doesn't work either. What about Power and prestige? Or, Religion? ...Everybody has an answer. But I happen to believe the Bible when it says, "There is a way that seems right to a person, but in the end, it produces death," Proverbs 14:12. Maybe we will never really be happy in this life. Well, it all depends on your idea of happiness.

However, I think there is an answer to the eternal question, "How do I find happiness and satisfaction in life?" Jesus stated the answer in our scripture – "I have come that they may have life, and have it to the full."

The good news is that not only did Jesus come to save us, but he also came to give us an abundant life. This is much like a second blessing: eternal life, plus "life to the full"! The hope of a wonderful, eternal life to come...and also an abundant life right here, right now.

What does the abundant life consist of? What would it look like to you? Let me tell you something I have learned from God's Word concerning people who really live and enjoy the abundant life - they will possess all of these qualities, and it will show: love, joy, peace, patience, kindness, goodness, faithfulness, gentleness, and self-control, all of which are the fruit of the Spirit. And, let me say one more thing about it; these are not individual fruit of which you can have one or two and not the others; this is the "fruit"- singular- of the Spirit. You don't live an abundant life if you have peace and kindness but no joy or love!

People who live and enjoy the abundant life also have compassion, humility, modesty, dignity, faith, character, wisdom, enthusiasm, optimism, confidence, honesty, and a vital and passionate relationship with God. They also have a passion for whatever they are doing. In other words, the abundant life is full of all the things money can't buy. No matter how much money you have, you cannot buy more patience, self-control, or salvation! You can't buy the desire or passion to do something. Hardware stores do not sell wisdom or hope. And, in case you are wondering, yes, you can possess all of these qualities! You can get everyone of these things from God, who is the giver of all good things.

But, remember that the "opposite of truth is also true". So, everyone who desires to live the abundant life avoids these negative qualities that are just the opposite and lead to an unhappy and unsatisfied life: selfishness, hatred, lust, unforgiveness, envy, jealousy, fear, drunkenness, sexual immorality, discord and malice, fits or rage, dishonesty, greed, gossiping, slander, pessimism, despair and self-pity. In other words, the more these negative qualities are a part of a person's behavior, the further they are from obtaining this "abundant life" that Jesus came to give.

God can remove all of these negative characteristics from a person's life. Every one of them! God is greater than our sins! Paul wrote in 1 Corinthians 6:11- "And this is what some of you *WERE*...But you were washed, you were sanctified, you were justified in the name of the Lord Jesus Christ and by the Spirit of our God."

So it's no longer an excuse to say, "This is who I am...this is just the way I am... and I can't change that; oh yes you can. Part of the abundant life is being able to make right decisions and follow through on them. Now there is no doubt, many non-Christians can experience some happiness and satisfaction in their lives, but that is usually because they <u>practice</u> some of the qualities that make up the abundant life, such as patience, integrity, and kindness, and a certain morality. They also <u>avoid </u>many of the things that destroy the abundant life which I also mention-ed. However, Jesus said that unless we believe in him, we will die in our sins, and the only thing we have to look forward to is judgment. We must, therefore, realize that no matter how much happiness a non-Christian seems to experience, it is unfortunately limited in quality and it's only temporary. You cannot be happy if you have no hope for the future. The facts are - anyone without the saving grace of Jesus, Christ in their life is spiritually dead. A person cannot live the "abundant life" if they are spiritually dead.

Many assume the abundant life depends on circumstances, or fate or luck, or their bank account, or their status in life, or their health, and, no doubt these things are highly valued in our lives; but wealth, power, status, worldly pleasure, and even health issues have nothing to do with living the abundant life Jesus came to give.

As we learn to see what life is all about, we will begin to see all around us many people who are successfully living this "life to the full" inspite of circumstances. These people quietly go about their lives filled with meaning and hope, happiness, satisfaction and vitality, and peace of mind. They enjoy quality friendships, have good, loving, family relationships, and a strong faith in God. Their life becomes an adventure worth living. They do not allow trivial or non-essential matters to control their thoughts and their life! Life is too short to waste time complaining, or arguing, or worrying about such things.

However, let me tell you what the abundant life is not:

#1. It is not necessarily a life of comfort and ease. Sometimes we need to "go through the fire" in order for it to melt away the impurities inside us. This is how God refines, and strengthens, and matures us.

There is a beautiful picture of abundance in the Old Testament story of Israel coming out of Egypt and into Canaan…God delivered them from bondage and tried to give them great abundance, but they were afraid of what it would cost them to get it. When they saw the giants in the land they decided that the whole journey had been some cruel trick, and it cost them abundant life. But, you see, Canaan does not represent heaven. I don't care how much we sing about crossing the Jordan, it was not heaven on the other side. Canaan is a picture of abundant life, but those who went over the Jordan River with Joshua fought for every inch of that land. Did God want to give it to them? Yes. Was it a land of milk and honey? You bet it was – but trusting in God they had to fight for every inch of it. Don't expect the abundant life to come easy. There are going to be giants in the way, and obstacles of some sort, but God desires for us to have the abundant life that Jesus came to give, and He will help us all along the way, if we let him.

#2. I have already mentioned once but it bears repeating; it is not dependent on outside circumstances. It's not what happens to you in this life that is nearly as important as how you respond to it.

#3. It is not glamorous, flashy or outwardly impressive. Fame or Fortune and million dollar homes and $500 suits are not where it is found. The abundant life is much like that small gate and narrow road that Jesus told us about in Matthew 7:13. The reason why so few will find it is because it takes more EFFORT to find it.

"I CAME THAT THEY MAY HAVE LIFE, AND HAVE IT MORE ABUNDANTLY". A few years from now, Lord willing, you are going to be a few years older. Either you will be a few years older and enjoying the abundant life, or you will be a few years older and still not get it!

In John 10:10, Jesus uses the Greek word "perissos" (pronounced per-is-sos'). In this context, it means 'superior in quantity or quality' 'exceedingly more' or 'very high' or a "great advantage' and 'beyond measure'. This is the exact same word that Paul uses in Ephesians 3:20 that you hear at the close of church services called a benediction: "Now to Him who is able to do <u>exceedingly</u> <u>abundantly</u> ("perissos") beyond all that we ask or think, according to the power that works within us." The abundant life is about a quality of life far exceeding what most people settle for, and it's available because Jesus came to make it available. But it takes effort on our part to discover what it really is for each one of us.

Matthew 7:7-14 – "Ask and it will be given to you; seek and you will find; knock and the door will be opened to you. For everyone who asks receives; the one who seeks finds; and to the one who knocks, the door will be opened.

"Which of you, if your son asks for bread, will give him a stone? Or if he asks for a fish, will give him a snake? If you, then, though you are evil, know how to give good gifts to your children, how much more will your Father in heaven give good gifts to those who ask him! So in everything, do to others what you would have them do to you, for this sums up the Law and the Prophets.

"Enter through the narrow gate. For wide is the gate and broad is the road that leads to destruction, and many enter through it. But small is the gate and narrow the road that leads to life, and only a few find it."

Being an electrician, it is easy for me to draw on the analogy of a "light" in the physical sense. One thing I know is that a light needs some source of power. And, if not connected to the right source, the light may be very dim, or not work at all. We, as Christians, have the greatest and most powerful source available to us to make our spiritual light shine like the "stars in the universe"…However, some Christians try to make their light shine by attempting to generate power by some other means…maybe works, or talents, or knowledge, but the key words here are "trying to make" their light shine. We ought to stop trying to make our light shine, and start "allowing" God's light to shine through us. We are called to reflect God's light, not try to create our own.

Paul tells us in our text for today, that it is "God who works in you to will and to act according to his good purpose" the problem is that we don't always "allow" Him to do so. As I read and re-read this scripture, I asked myself the question - "How does God work in me?" Does the Bible give us some idea of *how* God works in us to will and to act according to His good purpose? And of course, the answer is yes. So I would like to give you a few of the things I found.

The first has to do with <u>empowerment</u>; it is found in Ephesians 3:16-20 and it may be very familiar to you; "I pray that out of his glorious riches he may *strengthen you with <u>POWER</u> through His Spirit in your inner being*, so that Christ may dwell in your hearts through faith. And I pray that you, being rooted and established in love, may have *<u>POWER</u>* together with all the saints, to grasp how wide and how long and high and deep is the love of Christ, and to know this love that surpasses knowledge, that you may be filled to the measure of all the fullness of God. Now to Him who is able to do immeasurably more than we ask or imagine, according to *His <u>POWER</u> that is at work within us*...to Him be the glory!" Three times he mentions "power" so, first of all, God works in us to "empower" us.

The Christian life is not the easy life. It is not easy because it goes against the flow of the world. It's like trying to paddle upstream! In fact, I would say it is the most challenging lifestyle one can choose. When you "go with the flow, when you go downstream, you can just let the current of the world "float your boat"!

Not too far from where we lived in northern Wisconsin, is the Nemakagon River. One of the best things to do on a warm summer day was to float the river. It was about a three or four mile trip that took about 4 hours to complete. You could just sit back in an inner tube, and just float the day away! The current of the river would just take you downstream. Now, Jesus said; "Seek to enter the narrow gate, for narrow is the road and difficult is the path that leads to life and there are few who find it." Do you know that when the river is narrow - the current is stronger - and the paddling much harder! (That is if you are going upstream - against the flow)

One thing I have learned about this Christian lifestyle is that God will always call us to go beyond our limitations and step outside of our comfort zone. He will always call us to rise above our faults and our character flaws and weaknesses. It's only by God's empowerment that we can live this abundant, fulfilling, rewarding life He offers. And, when we choose to go upstream, He will work in us and empower us to will and to act according to His good purpose; because, greater is He who is in you than he who is in the world! God empowers.

Secondly, I find that - like a potter, God works in us to form us, mold us, and make us into the vessel He created us to be. In my book "Jars of Clay" I wrote about this subject. Some of us are created to be beautiful vases and some of us are created to be jars, and some are created to just be plain old POTS! However we must remember that there are many different kinds of pots, and each has a unique purpose. The story is of course found in Jeremiah 18 - God sends

Jeremiah to the potter's house to learn a lesson as he tells him "Like clay in the hand of the potter, so you are in my hand" God is at work within us to mold us and make us to will and to act according to <u>His</u> good purpose; not <u>ours</u>! While a crystal vase may be beautiful, it can't strain spaghetti! My point is this; we can only be useful to God if we allow Him to work in us to become what H<u>e intended</u> for us to be.

Third, I find that God gives each one of us Spiritual gifts, and talents and skills. And, God works in us to use those gifts to fulfill our part in the ministry of his church. 1 Corinthians 12:4 - "There are different kinds of gifts, but the same Spirit. There are different kinds of service, but the same Lord. There are different kinds of working, but the *same God works all of them in all men.* Now to each one the manifestation of the Spirit is given for the common good." And, in Ephesians 4:11 - "It was He who gave some to be apostles, some to be prophets, some to be evangelists, and some to be pastors and teachers, to prepare God's people for works of service, so that the body of Christ may be built up." This is just a partial list. Each one of us has a part to play in the ministry of the church, and God has enabled us to do our part, whatever that may be.

Paul also uses the analogy of the human body to show that the church is made up of many parts, all of which are needed for the body to function properly. God does not desire for us to ever be envious of someone else or their role in the church; nor does He desire for us to be critical of others in the church; and we especially should not be critical of someone else if we are not fulfilling our role. In fact, we ought to remember that if one part of the body is <u>not</u> functioning, the rest of the body has to work twice as hard to overcome the handicap! (Think about it.)

So, let's look at this whole thing, this whole scripture together: God has created us to be a part of the body of Christ; and He has also given us a purpose in the body of Christ; therefore, He is forever working in us - molding and shaping our lives through circumstances and experiences - to prepare us to fulfill that purpose; however large or small that purpose may be. He also works in us to empower us and enable us with gifts and talents and skills, to will and to act according to His purpose - *as we work out our salvation-* in order to get the very most out of life as we possibly can; so we can Shine! Shine! Shine in the world around us. You see, it's a partnership. As we "work out our salvation" God works in us at the same time, and the result is - we reap the greatest potential possible from this short earthly life.

"Six Ways to Grow In Assurance"

#1. - "Walking In The Light"

Ephesians 5:8-13 – "For you were once darkness, but now you are light in the Lord. Live as children of light (for the fruit of the light consists in all goodness, righteousness and truth) and find out what pleases the Lord. Have nothing to do with the fruitless deeds of darkness, but rather expose them. It is shameful even to mention what the disobedient do in secret. But everything exposed by the light becomes visible—and everything that is illuminated becomes a light."

1 John 1:5-7 – "This is the message we have heard from him and declare to you: God is light; in him there is no darkness at all. If we claim to have fellowship with him and yet walk in the darkness, we lie and do not live out the truth. But if we walk in the light, as he is in the light, we have fellowship with one another, and the blood of Jesus, his Son, purifies us from all sin."

I want us to look at the subject of "light".

The writings of the Apostle John - are the last four books of the Bible; plus his Gospel. John sums up his gospel in John 20:31 with the words; "These things are written that you may believe that Jesus is the Christ, the Son of God, and that by believing you may have life in his name." The Book of Revelation has its purpose in the very first verse; "The revelation of Jesus Christ, which God gave him to show his servants what must soon take place." Revelation is a book concerned with the "end times" the "last days" things of the future. And then, there is 1st, 2nd, and 3rd John, where he writes in 5:13 - "I write these things to you who believe" - that is Christians – those who now believe; "so that you may <u>KNOW</u> that you have eternal life"…That's assurance!

In this letter of 1st. John, I find at least 8 ways that we can "know" or have the assurance of eternal life. The assurance that "in and through Christ" we have and are walking in "fellowship with God" and can be at peace, knowing that our name is in the Lamb's book; and heaven is our home!

First of all it's important to know that John is not just giving his opinion here as to how we ought to live and grow, for he says in the very first verse; and watch the progression here; "That which we have "heard", that which we have "seen", (or we could say that which we have "read" or "looked at" or "studied") "and our hands have touched" (personal experience) "This is what we proclaim to you!" You see, John was there! He heard Jesus, he saw Jesus, and he touched Jesus! He tells us of his experience by summing it up in the words - "God is light!"

John pulls no punches in this letter. For one, he uses the verb tense of the word "walk" which means to "keep on walking"…it is an action. If we keep on walking, we have continual fellowship. I cannot stand in one place and say I am walking; it involves forward movement or progress. Walking is however harder than talking about walking. I can sit in an easy chair and talk about walking. I can even talk the language of walking, but until I actually walk, it has little value. John uses the same reasoning here, "If we say we have fellowship with Him, but are not walking in the light, we lie!" In other words, if we claim to be a Christian, but there is no sign of motion or movement or growth, John says we lie.

Do you know that even the greatest scientists are baffled by the mystery of light? They can study it and explain the effects of it, but they still don't understand what light is! Hmmm…John simply says; "God is light" and he is just as mysterious in the spiritual sense as light is in the natural to scientists.

An October 2001 edition of the National Geographic had an amazing article on the "Power of Light." This is what the introduction said; "Light reveals the world to us. Body and soul crave it. Light sets our biological clock. It triggers in our brains to the sensations of color. It feeds us by supplying the energy needed for growth. Light inspires us with special effects like rainbows, sunrises and sunsets. It gives us life-changing tools, from light bulbs - to lasers - to fiber optics. Scientists don't fully understand what light is or what the limitless possibilities are…They just know that it will illuminate our future!" (Hello!)

Let me take just a moment to compare that with knowing God; It says in John 8:12 - "When Jesus spoke again to the people, he said, "I am the light of the world. Whoever follows me will never walk in darkness, but will have the "light" of life!" You see, knowing God, who is light, reveals to us the world as it really is.

Light is essential to our lives. When you don't have light, or you are without light for an extended period of time, sadness and depression set in and growth is stifled!

*God, who is light, triggers the sensation of color in our brains and we are able to see the beauty of all that he has created for our enjoyment!

*God who is light has given us many tools to show us the unlimited power of light! Listen to this; Fiber optic cables, when pulsated with infrared light can transmit ten million phone conversations at one time! Now, if one fiber optic cable of light can do that, how is it that God can hear the prayers of millions of people at the same time? Because God is light! Lasers are available for everything from surgery to stopping missiles from space! ...and...God Is Light!

*Finally, the article says that scientists know that light will illuminate our future! John knows, and you and I know that when you come into God's light, he illuminates our future! This is worth getting excited over!

John talks about "walking in the light." Light enables us to work; it produces growth; it reveals beauty and provides safety; light represents what is good, pure, holy, and true. Is it any wonder why Jesus tells us to "let our light shine?" Light also exposes. In the dark, good and evil look alike; it's hard to distinguish something in the dark. In the light they can be distinguished! You can tell the difference. If you want to know where you are going, "walk in the light" says Jesus...that's Assurance."

Let me address one more thing in closing; What happens when I sin after I am a Christian? Do I all of a sudden stop being a Christian? Do I have to start all over again? John's answer in verse seven is "No" - "But, if we walk in the light as he himself is in the light, we have fellowship with one another" - NOW, watch this –

"and the blood of Jesus his Son cleanses us from all sin." Notice the little two letter word "IF" in those two scriptures; "IF we walk in the light" and "IF we confess our sins". We have a responsibility in this process, and IF we do our part, He will do his!

Let me use the example of the child learning to walk; "Oops, he fell"...Do we condemn the child? No, we know that as long as the child keeps trying and practicing, it will eventually learn to walk. And, as the child continues to grow, he will even learn to run and jump and climb. Have you ever watched a child learning to walk? When they are learning to walk, what do they do with their arms? (Hold them high)

The new twenty dollar bills are out. How many have had a good look at them? Just a few days after they came out there were counterfeits on the street. It is interesting that a new twenty dollar bill has all kinds of anti-counterfeiting things on it. They've got colors. The number "twenty" is in a kind of a gold paint. They've got a blue eagle on it and if you hold it up to the light you can see another picture of Andrew Jackson; kind of a watermark. Of course, there's always the plastic strip that's embedded up in the corner or the whole width of the bill, and a color copier can't see that. So, if you have a twenty dollar bill you have a lot of ways to tell whether it's real. You can hold it up to light and if it's been copied, then you'll see all kinds of things missing! Let me repeat that again, in case you were sleeping; "You can hold it up to the light and see if it is a counterfeit, because you will see a lot of things missing!"

Walking in the light gives us assurance.

1 John 2:3-5 – "We know that we have come to know him if we keep his commands. Whoever says, "I know him," but does not do what he commands is a liar, and the truth is not in that person. But if anyone obeys his word, love for God[a] is truly made complete in them. This is how we know we are in him:

James 1:19-25 – "My dear brothers and sisters, take note of this: Everyone should be quick to listen, slow to speak and slow to become angry, because human anger does not produce the righteousness that God desires. Therefore, get rid of all moral filth and the evil that is so prevalent and humbly accept the word planted in you, which can save you.

Do not merely listen to the word, and so deceive yourselves. Do what it says. Anyone who listens to the word but does not do what it says is like someone who looks at his face in a mirror and, after looking at himself, goes away and immediately forgets what he looks like. But whoever looks intently into the perfect law that gives freedom, and continues in it—not forgetting what they have heard, but doing it—they will be blessed in what they do."

One of Satan's favorite tactics is to cause us to question whether we indeed are in fellowship with God. John counters that with some great identifying marks and the first one is this; are you walking in the light? Remember that the one word John uses a lot here is "continues." We must be continuously in the light! Jesus said, we must "remain" in the vine, not just be in the vine once in a while, or whenever we feel like it, or just when it's appropriate; not just "step into the light" on Sundays; but continuously!

The second is, "Are you walking in obedience?" Somewhere along the line people have the mistaken idea that salvation is without obligation. However, John says in verse three - "We know we have come to know Him," and now here's the if "if we obey His commands." In other words, we know that we have come to know him, we have the security, the assurance, because we have seen in our lives the change that has taken place so that;

*The commands we once thought were ridiculous and stupid and life-destroying, we now learn to joyfully obey... because God's work in our lives changes our understanding.

*We have come to learn that this God who we used to hate, we now love.

*And the commands that we used to disregard and were "not for me", have now become something we follow.

What can explain a psalmist writing, "Oh, how I love your law! I meditate on it all day long." Does that sound like something a typical non-believer would say? No. This is a person who has been changed, who's understood that the God he hated and feared is in fact a God of tremendous love and has embraced him and brought him into fellowship with Him and he says, "Man, I love your law! The lights are on, the blinders are off, and now I can see how wonderful your Word and your commands are." "If anyone obeys His word," verse 5 says, "God's love is truly made complete in him." Not - will be made complete, IS made complete! This obedience or "keeping of God's Word" means we are actively complying with His Word. It means we habitually keep or keep on keeping His commandments. What I know does not mean a whole lot unless it leads me down the path of obedience.

This is not something based on feelings; I can't just "feel" like I am a Christian; or "feel" like I know where my eternal destiny is...no, John says absolute assurance comes from a clear understanding of the facts. Back in the "good ole days" there was a show called Dragnet, and whenever a witness would begin to ramble on about something, Sgt. Friday would always say; "Just the facts Maam, just the facts." John says, the fact is that "We know that we have come to know Him if we are walking in obedience."

That does not mean that our lives are characterized by total, perfect obedience...there is only one that is perfect, but that our lives will be characterized by a consistent and continual desire to do what is right and good according to God's Word. In other words, there will be more than just "hearing and reading" God's Word, there will be a desire to "understand and apply" what we know. And, when this is happening in our lives, Romans 8:16 tells us that the "Spirit himself bears witness with our spirit that we are children of God."

John is very blunt and to the point in verse 4 when he says; "the man who says "I know Him" but does not do what He commands is a liar, and the truth is not in him." This is the second time John has told us to quit lying to ourselves! In verse 3 the words "that we have *come to* know him" suggests a growing process. In that process we "come to know" more about God; we "come to know" more about Jesus; we "come to know" more of His Word; and we "come to know" what He desires of us; and we come to obey! That's what brings assurance. Not out of fear or force, but a true desire to please God and obey as a result of a loving relationship.

I like to put it this way; "Being a Christian is a "Be" experience; "Believing"; "Becoming"; and "Behaving" all of which are a part of "obedience". Believing is the first step to Becoming and Behaving, and Becoming and Behaving are the direct results of believing! I think John would agree that if there is no becoming and behaving, there really is no believing!

Assurance comes from obedience to his commands…such as; Matthew 4:19 "And he saith unto them, Follow me, and I will make you fishers of men." There are too many Christians who are no longer "fishers of men" but "keepers of the aquarium!"

In Matthew 25:6 -10 we read, "And at midnight there was a cry made, Behold, the bridegroom comes; go ye out to meet him. And they that were ready went in with him to the marriage: and the door was shut." I believe that we are living on the threshold of that midnight cry. For many, the door will soon be shut. Now is the time - the time for those without Christ to come to Christ! Now is the time for those who are in darkness to step into the light!

1 John 2:6 – "Whoever claims to live in him must live as Jesus did."

Ephesians 5:1-2 – "Follow God's example, therefore, as dearly loved children and walk in the way of love, just as Christ loved us and gave himself up for us as a fragrant offering and sacrifice to God."

Ephesians 5:8-10 and 15-17 – "For you were once darkness, but now you are light in the Lord. Live as children of light (for the fruit of the light consists in all goodness, righteousness and truth) and find out what pleases the Lord. Have nothing to do with the fruitless deeds of darkness, but rather expose them. It is shameful even to mention what the disobedient do in secret. But everything exposed by the light becomes visible—and everything that is illuminated becomes a light. This is why it is said: "Wake up, sleeper, rise from the dead, and Christ will shine on you."

Be very careful, then, how you live—not as unwise but as wise, making the most of every opportunity, because the days are evil. Therefore do not be foolish, but understand what the Lord's will is."

When it comes to the Christian walk with God, the world sees it as a lifestyle of negatives; "You can't do this"…"You don't do that" "You "shouldn't go here or there" and it's also filled with a lot of "have to's" You "have to attend church." "You have to give 10% of your income." "You have to stop doing anything that's fun!" But, when I read my Bible, I see all the things that Jesus did! It doesn't list the things that he didn't do! And, even our text for today does not say "Don't do the things that Jesus didn't do"; it says "If you want the assurance that Christ is in you and the assurance that you are growing as a Christian, then do the things he did!

I want to give you a list of the positive actions that Jesus took and that we can take, in order to walk in his steps. All these spring from the transforming love of God in our lives. When God changes someone and they surrender to Him, they will begin to walk like Jesus walked. They will begin to think and act like Jesus thought and acted. There will be a noticeable difference in their lives that only the presence of God's Holy Spirit can bring. Jesus himself said in John 14:12 "I tell you the truth, anyone who has faith in me will do what I have been doing…And even greater things than these."

1st. Peter 2:21 tells us "To this you were called, because Christ suffered for you, leaving you an example, that you should follow in his steps." Jesus said the same thing in John 13:15 - "I have set you an example that you should do as I have done for you."

So, if we are to walk as Jesus walked, we need to know what that walk consists of. What was it about Jesus that we are to bring into or apply to our lives as well?

#1. Jesus walked with Compassion.

Mark 6:34 says that "when Jesus saw the crowds, he had compassion on them, because they were like sheep without a shepherd. So he began to teach them…" Compassion is an emotion that moves us to take some kind of action. It is not pity, because we can have pity on someone without doing anything, but compassion moves or motivates us to take action. In the case of the scripture I just mentioned, it says that Jesus began to teach them. In compassion he saw that they were "lost" they were wandering around in life with no real understanding; no real knowledge of truth. We live in an age of selfishness and apathy to the physical and the spiritual needs of others. It's a "look out for number one" mentality; or a "Let someone else worry about it" mentality; or even a "We have organizations and even a government that can take care of that" mentality. Jesus says we need to walk in compassion as he walked in compassion.

#2. Jesus walked in Power.

In Luke 8:18 it says "The Spirit of the Lord is upon me, because he has anointed me to preach the good news to the poor. He has sent me to proclaim freedom for the prisoners; and recovery of sight to the blind; to release the oppressed; to proclaim the year of the Lord's favor!" We Christ-ians sometimes act as though what we have to say to people is like a "bitter pill" rather than good news! We need to walk in the power and authority of the Gospel of Christ given by Almighty God! We need to recognize and use the power available to us in the Spirit of God. It's time we, as the church, stop walking in intimidation and fear, and start walking in the confidence that we profess to have in the God whom we serve! He is who He says He is! And He can do what He says He can do!

#3. Jesus walked in humility.

Even though he had the power of a million angels at his side, Jesus walked in humility. He became a servant. He always had a non-selfish attitude that looked to the needs of others and put others first. He never used his power in a forceful way, but humbly put his own needs and desires aside, in order to bless those with a real need. Humility requires sacrifice; and if we are to walk as Jesus walked, we will be called to sacrifice.

#4. Jesus walked in Knowledge.

One of the greatest problems that has always existed in the church is the problem of Bible illiteracy. There are too many Christians who won't witness to others because of a fear that they will ask them something about the Bible that they don't know or can't answer. So, rather than look stupid, they just don't do it. If we are to walk as Jesus walked, we must have a thorough knowledge of God's Word. We need to know and believe - as 2 Peter 1:3 says - that the Bible contains "everything we need for life and godliness through our knowledge of Him." We need to know and understand the many precious promises of God; we need to "add to our faith knowledge" it says; and in an ever increasing measure! This will keep you from being "ineffective and unproductive!" "Always be ready to give an answer" is the Bible's admonishment to us if we are to walk as Jesus walked.

#5. Jesus walked in Unity.

Jesus was united with the Father in heart, purpose, mind, and will. And, he wants us to walk in that unity as well. Not in a unity that say we can't have a difference of opinions, or that we all think and act alike; that's not what he's talking about. But rather it's a unity that comes from understanding and experiencing the love and power of God; It's a unity that understands what it means to be in the world but not of the world; It's a unity that knows and understands the truth of God's Word and its value in life; It's a unity that shares the desire to offer the world the free gift, and the option of, eternal life through Jesus Christ who is the only way of salvation; so they can make an intelligent decision of their own freewill. It's a unity of a common and shared doctrine within the true church of Christ. If we are to walk as Jesus walked, we will be united in these things. And, finally, #6. Jesus walked in Expectancy.

Jesus expected people to change. Jesus expected people to be healed. Jesus expected people to be delivered from addictions and abuse. Jesus expected God the Father to answer prayer and to do the unexpected! And, Jesus expects us to walk in that same expectancy as his followers. We need to believe God! We need to believe that God can change and transform even the worst of sinners. We have no right to pick and choose who we think ought to be a part of Christ's church because he expects all to be a part! It is God's will that not one should perish! We need to walk believing that "nothing is impossible with God."

John says in 5:13 - "I write these things to you who believe in the name of the Son of God, so that you may know (have the assurance of) "eternal life." Are you walking in His steps? Are you walking with compassion? Are you walking in power? Are you walking in humility at the same time? Are you walking in unity of one heart and mind with Jesus? Are you walking with expectancy?

1 John 2:15-17 – "Do not love the world or anything in the world. If anyone loves the world, love for the Father is not in them. For everything in the world—the lust of the flesh, the lust of the eyes, and the pride of life—comes not from the Father but from the world. The world and its desires pass away, but whoever does the will of God lives forever."

John 17:13-19 – "I am coming to you now, but I say these things while I am still in the world, so that they may have the full measure of my joy within them. I have given them your word and the world has hated them, for they are not of the world any more than I am of the world. My prayer is not that you take them out of the world but that you protect them from the evil one. They are not of the world, even as I am not of it. Sanctify them by the truth; your word is truth. As you sent me into the world, I have sent them into the world. For them I sanctify myself, that they too may be truly sanctified."

Definition of Worldliness: Worldliness is the lust of the flesh (a passion for sensual satisfaction), the lust of the eyes (a constant desire for the finer things of life), and the pride of life (self-satisfaction in who we are, what we have, and what we have done. Sort of a puffed up view of ourselves compared to others.) Worldliness elevates creature comfort to the point of idolatry; with contentment never to found. Too many people think that worldliness is something limited to external behavior. Others think worldliness is hanging out with the wrong kinds of people. Worldliness is a wrong attitude of the heart that indicates a lack of a totally consuming love and trust for the Lord.

It has been said that there are Nine Marks of Worldliness - and they all start with the letter "P" - pride, selfish pleasures, possessions, popularity, power, position, people pleasing, and privilege (all of which are for selfish reasons.)

The Bible uses the word "world" in various different ways:

* The physical planet…mountains, tree, grass, rivers, etc.

* The people on the planet.

* False religions, lifestyles & values and attitudes in opposition to God and His Word…this is what John means by the "world" here.

Someone once said that "living for the world is like rearranging the furniture on the Titanic." The Titanic IS going down. The Bible says "This world and all therein is doomed to destruction" as well.

One of the things I haven't done since leaving Wisconsin is fishing. I love to fish; and some of the best fishing is in Wisconsin. There I had 27 lakes within a 20 minute drive of my first church. I had several poles and reels for different types of fishing, and a tackle box. A tackle box of course is filled with lures. The world in which we live is filled with lures that Satan uses to lure us away from God. He entices us, and tempts us, and points to our natural or fleshly desires and says "Come on, you know you really want this!" What are the characteristics of a lure? They are brightly colored; attractive; some with spinners for added attraction. If you are hungry, it offers fulfillment; If you are bored, it offers excitement; If you are sick & tired, it offers to make you feel better; It offers pleasure and satisfaction. The problem with lures is the hooks! I have noticed that sometimes, when the fish realizes it is hooked, it fights and fights, and if it is strong enough, it breaks the line, but sometimes the hook is too deep.

In these three verses it is God, through the pen of John, who points out three of the world's best lures. These are the ones used most often and with the most success, that have earned the right to be in the top of the tackle box! They have hooked more fish than any others;

1. The "cravings of sinful man" (whatever makes me happy and a self-indulgent desire to be #1 no matter what I have to do to get there.)

2. The lure of the "lust of the eyes"…which can be a couple of things; (A pre-occupation with physical desires) - (the lure of materialism or craving and accumulating things - which is covetousness.)

3. The lure of "pride" or "boasting" (whatever makes me look good, and seeks reward, and whether purposely or not, puts others down.) These are Satan's three best lures.

Most people have the idea that "worldliness" is external; in other words something we can see, the people we associate with, the places we go, or the things we participate in, or even the things we have. However, these things - maybe because they are external things - are "legalistic". In other words they are an adherence to certain manmade rules or conduct, in order to live up to mans idea of what a Christian looks and acts like. But, the truth of God's Word tells us that while "man sees the outside or external things, God sees the heart." We have a tendency to look at what a person may have or what a person may do, and say "Surely they can't be a Christian." Just because they have a lot of things; or just because they wear flashy clothes; or just because they play cards or go dancing or don't fit our mold in some other way. "God sees the heart" means that He knows our attitude toward these things, and He knows if they are "of the world". So, we must start not by looking at outward symptoms, but by digging down to our very hearts, and looking there. What are the desires of my heart? What does my heart find satisfaction in, and what do I put my confidence in, and what brings me comfort? Is it in this temporary earthly life and the things that belong to it? Or, is it in God and His blessing and plan and purpose for my life and the life to come?

When we become Christians and understand the things of God, we read things like Paul telling us we must "put off the old self" and we need to remember that he also says "and put on the new self". If we give up or "put off" something in our lives, it leaves a void, and if we do not fill that void with something else, Satan will constantly tempt us to re-fill it with the things of the world. We call that "backsliding." So, we if we give up worldly attitudes, we must fill up with Godly attitudes. If we put off worldly thinking, we need to put on godly thinking, and so on. So, as we've seen, love for the world and love for God cannot mix; they do not, and cannot, live together in the same spirit. Again, only God fits in that God-shaped hole. Love for the world and love of God are like oil and water; they're like twinkies and broccoli; things that just don't go together. We cannot truly love God and love the world at the same time. Jesus said in Matthew 6:24: "No one can serve two masters." Either he will hate the one and love the other, or he will be devoted to one and despise the other." Let me put it this way; "It is right for the church to be in the world; it is wrong for the world to be in the church. (I am speaking of worldly attitudes and thinking.) A boat in the water is good; that is what boats are for; however, water inside the boat causes it to sink. Love for the world pushes out love for God, but the opposite is also true; a love for God will and should, push out love for the world."

In verse 17, John gives us two clues as to why this is important to us. First, he says; because "the world and its desires pass away." Things in and of this world die, rust and moth destroy, they get old, they wear out, they are stolen, or lost, and as we have seen, as in a tornado, they are destroyed by nature itself and gone in an instant. How important are things, and fame or fortune, when life is on the line?

Second, he says "the man who does the will of God lives forever." In other words, it's the eternal things - the things done for God - and out of love for God - the treasures in heaven - that are truly important. It is not wrong to have things, it is wrong when things have you! It's not wrong to be wealthy, it's wrong when decisions and attitudes are influenced by wealth rather than God. It is not wrong to desire better things in life, it is wrong when the success of our lives is defined by the world's view and not by God's view.

So, basically, it comes down to a look within, to see what God sees. If our desires and motives are selfish and worldly; it could mean that we have been hooked. We need to recognize the lures of the world for what they really are, and learn to see the hook! Take home this thought with you today; "God is able and will provide for our every need. His Word even says he will "give us the desires of our hearts" but, God will never tempt us in any way. James 1:13 reads - "When tempted, no one should say, "God is tempting me" For God cannot be tempted by evil, nor does he tempt anyone but each one is tempted when by his own evil desire, he is dragged away and enticed." I say, learn to see the hook!

1st. John 3:1-10 – "See what great love the Father has lavished on us, that we should be called children of God! And that is what we are! The reason the world does not know us is that it did not know him. Dear friends, now we are children of God, and what we will be has not yet been made known. But we know that when Christ appears, we shall be like him, for we shall see him as he is. All who have this hope in him purify themselves, just as he is pure.

Everyone who sins breaks the law; in fact, sin is lawlessness. But you know that he appeared so that he might take away our sins. And in him is no sin. No one who lives in him keeps on sinning. No one who continues to sin has either seen him or known him.

Dear children, do not let anyone lead you astray. The one who does what is right is righteous, just as he is righteous. The one who does what is sinful is of the devil, because the devil has been sinning from the beginning. The reason the Son of God appeared was to destroy the devil's work. No one who is born of God will continue to sin, because God's seed remains in them; they cannot go on sinning, because they have been born of God. This is how we know who the children of God are and who the children of the devil are: Anyone who does not do what is right is not God's child, nor is anyone who does not love their brother and sister."

Mark 9:42-47 – "If anyone causes one of these little ones—those who believe in me—to stumble, it would be better for them if a large millstone were hung around their neck and they were thrown into the sea. If your hand causes you to stumble, cut it off. It is better for you to enter life maimed than with two hands to go into hell, where the fire never goes out. And if your foot causes you to stumble, cut it off. It is better for you to enter life crippled than to have two feet and be thrown into hell. And if your eye causes you to stumble, pluck it out. It is better for you to enter the kingdom of God with one eye than to have two eyes and be thrown into hell,"

Once again, I have been writing about assurance. In John's first letter, he gives us eight ways that we can tell, or know, or have the assurance that we are a child of God; saved by grace and walking in righteousness. What I would like to do this morning is put together, or bring together verses six and nine of our text, and see if we can decipher what John means when he says; "No one who is born of God will continue to sin." He basically says the same thing three times in these verses; "No one who lives in Him keeps on sinning"..."No one who continues to sin has either seen Him or knows Him" And, of course, "No one who is born of God will continue to sin." Then he tells us why this is so at the end of verse 9 - "because God's seed remains in him; he _**cannot**_ **go on sinning, because he has been born of God.**" This is how we know! Says John.

In order to clarify something in our own minds, let me first explain what John does not mean; He does not mean that Christians do not or cannot sin..."never say never". What I hope will come across is the <u>difference between committing sin - and continuing in sin.</u> If we are to understand more fully, we first have to know what our assurance is based on, and why we need it. The truth of verse 1 - that we are God's children, is only the beginning, and the future we face as His children is far beyond our human comprehension. God has revealed however, that when the Lord returns, Christ's work of redemption will be complete in us; and "we shall be like him." Our resurrection bodies will be like his glorified body...our moral likeness will match his, and the process that began when we first came to the Cross, when we first came to know Christ, will be consummated and we will be fully and completely sanctified! This is our blessed hope! That "He who began a good work in us will be faithful to complete it!" Anyone who has this hope will be motivated toward moral and spiritual growth, with the ultimate goal of being "holy as He is holy!" It's the assurance of the life to come; the life eternal. I pray you can say that you have this assurance today!

I could explain what John is trying to tell us in this way; If God lives in us and we in Him, then our lives will be characterized by a constant and consistent walk away from sin and toward righteousness. Commentators have difficulty with these verses, when John says believers "do not sin" in verse six - and, "cannot sin" in verse nine. This is evidenced in the fact that they offer at least eight different views or interpretations of these verses. I am not going to confuse you this morning by listing all eight interpretations, I'll just give you the right one! It can be explained in a word; *Incompatible*.

What John is telling us is not the impossibility of sin, but rather, it's incompatibility with our "new nature". For you see, if we are born again, if we are a child of God, if we have come to Christ, the Bible says we have "put on the new self" "Old things have passed away, and all things become new." What this new self, this new nature, does not do, and cannot do, is "continue in" habitual and persistent sin.

A believer may sin, even with the consent of the mind and the will, but because of the indwelling Holy Spirit, he is always overwhelmed with grief and repentance, and does not continue in sin. SIN AND HOLINESS ARE INCOMPATIBLE!

Every one of us has areas where temptation is strong and habits are hard to conquer, but John is not talking about the Christian who does not yet have victory over that area of their lives. What he is talking about are those who make a practice of sinning while professing to be Christians - and in fact, look for ways to justify their sin! Even to the extent of saying "Well, I just don't have victory over that yet." John says, God is not in you if you continually try to justify sin in your life.

When we are truly born again, the Holy Spirit gives us a new nature, a new way of thinking, a new way of living, a new way of believing, and acting, a heart that seeks to be Christlike, and that - says John - is incompatible with sin! Paul suggests the same thing in Romans 8:5 where he says "those who live in accordance with the Spirit have their minds set on what the Spirit desires and their hearts set on what the Spirit desires." If we don't have that kind of mindset, John says God is not in us. And, he goes on to say; "the Spirit of God helps us to "put off the old self which is being corrupted by its deceitful desires; and to be made new in the attitude of our minds; and to put on the new self created to be like God in true righteousness and holiness." We come to know what God desires, and we "do not continue in sin."

Let me take a bold step here and suggest that this is - of all the areas John mentions - the area that we can discern the truth of our walk. Hear John's voice again; "No one who is born of God will continue to sin, because God's seed remains in him; He cannot go on sinning because he has been born of God." An unmarried man and woman for example, cannot continue to live together; it's incompatible! A bar owner cannot continue in business, it's incompatible! I hesitate to use any more examples, so as not to point the finger at any particular sin...sin is sin whether big or small, noticeable or unnoticeable. A born again child of God cannot walk in the light and walk in darkness at the same time! That person cannot walk with God and walk with the world at the same time. Nor can they be partially obedient...John says "No one who continues to sin has either seen Him or known Him." The reason is just that simple; there is no real repentance! And, without repentance, there is no atonement, and without atonement, there is no indwelling of the Holy Spirit, because the Spirit of God is "incompatible" with sin!

Let me close by repeating something I said earlier; John is talking about those who make a practice of continuing in sin - whatever that sin may be - while professing to be a born again, Spirit filled, Christian. It is not impossible for Christians to sin; however, the guilt and conviction of the Holy Spirit make it impossible to continue in unrepentant sin. It is incompatible with our new nature!

1 John 3:24 – "The one who keeps God's commands lives in him, and he in them. And this is how we know that he lives in us: We know it by the Spirit he gave us.

The key work of the Holy Spirit is:
1. To *TEACH* us and *REMIND* us.
2. To *CONVICT* us in regard to sin and righteousness and judgment.
3. To *TESTIFY* with our spirit, that we are children of God.
4. To manifest the *FRUIT* of the Spirit in our lives.
5. To give us *SPIRITUAL DISCERNMENT*
6. To *FILL* us, or take *CONTROL* of our lives... which the Bible calls the sanctification process.
7. All of this is to help us know that He is greater than Satan or the world.

"And, this is how we KNOW that He lives in us; we know by the Spirit he gave us." Once we understand these functions or the work or the purposes of the Holy Spirit in our lives, we then can look at ourselves and see if any of these things are there or not there in our lives.

It would be sad to find ourselves in the position of 1Corinthians 2:14 where the things of the Spirit are foolishness and we cannot understand the things that are spiritually discerned and, the only thing that applies our life is the fact that the Holy Spirit is constantly convicting of the guilt of sin! If that is true for you, I have some bad news, and some wonderful news for you this morning; The bad news is that the reason you may struggle spiritually is because the Holy Spirit has been stifled in your life, and the good news is that relief and joy and understanding and assurance, is only a prayer away!

You see, the Bible says that before coming to God through Christ, we are without the Spirit. Let me go back to 1 Corinthians 2:8-10 that says "no eye, ear, or mind can conceive what God has prepared for those who love Him." The fact is that our eye can't see it! Our ear can't hear it! Our mind cannot even imagine it! But, our spirit, now that's a different story! "God has revealed it to us by His Spirit." They are revealed in God's Word and the Holy Spirit in turn reveals these things to our spirit, and gives us the assurance that takes away all doubt and fear. The rest of that scripture reads; "The man without the Spirit does not accept the things that come from the Spirit of God" (Like a T.V. or a radio, the problem is not in the transmission of the Word, the problem is the receiver) "the things of the Spirit are foolishness him, and he cannot understand them, for they are spiritually discerned."

The mind is known as the "seat of intellect and knowledge". The heart is the "seat of emotion". Both are filled with good and bad, right and wrong. For many of us, even after being "born again" the mind and the heart - the intellect and the emotions - are still controlled by "SELF" and although self is able to discern good from bad, and right from wrong, self discerns pleasure and not truth! Romans chapter 8:8 calls this living by the flesh or "according to the sinful nature." You see, it all depends on who is sitting on the throne! Verse 9 goes on to say "You, however, are not controlled by the sinful nature, but by the Spirit, if the Spirit of God lives in you"... However, this is not just an automatic action on the part of the Holy Spirit, it is a voluntary reaction of the will; a reaction of our will to the prompting or leading of the Spirit. Verse 12 of Romans 8 says "Therefore, we have an obligation - to live by the Spirit, and put to death the deeds of the flesh"…Why? Because the Spirit discerns truth and not pleasure!

The Spirit teaches us truth, and reminds us of truth when we are tempted to yield to "self" or the "flesh." The Spirit convicts us of guilt, when and if, we do fall, and helps us to focus on repentance, forgiveness, and the future. Helping us to keep our eyes on eternity and eternal things, rather than just the things of this world. The Holy Spirit of God will only do in our lives that which we ask Him and allow Him to do.

In Romans 12:2 the Apostle Paul admonishes us "in view of God's mercy, to offer ourselves as living sacrifices, holy and pleasing to God; this is our spiritual act of worship; Do not conform any longer to the pattern of this world, but be transformed by the renewing of your mind." Now, listen to this - I know you have heard this many times - "Then, you will be able to TEST and APPROVE of what God's will is - His good, pleasing, and perfect will." If our lives are controlled, filled, led by the Holy Spirit; if the Spirit is on the "throne" of our minds and our emotions, and we are listening to the Spirit, then we can "test and approve" of those things in our lives that are according to God's will…and "put to death" as Paul puts it, those things that are not. It is an ongoing process that is changing the way we think, changing the way we feel, and ultimately, changing the way we act.

How can we know that we are children of God? I would say we must look at John, who basically is saying; "Look at your life and your lifestyle, and see who is on the throne! We will know by the spirit He gave us. Are you walking with the Spirit? Are you keeping in step with the Spirit? Ultimately, He will give the assurance we need!

1Timothy 2:1-4 – "I urge, then, first of all, that petitions, prayers, intercession and thanksgiving be made for all people— for kings and all those in authority, that we may live peaceful and quiet lives in all godliness and holiness. This is good, and pleases God our Savior, who wants all people to be saved and to come to a knowledge of the truth."

1 John 5:13-17 – "I write these things to you who believe in the name of the Son of God so that you may know that you have eternal life. This is the confidence we have in approaching God: that if we ask anything according to his will, he hears us. And if we know that he hears us—whatever we ask—we know that we have what we asked of him.

If you see any brother or sister commit a sin that does not lead to death, you should pray and God will give them life. I refer to those whose sin does not lead to death. There is a sin that leads to death. I am not saying that you should pray about that. All wrongdoing is sin, and there is sin that does not lead to death."

While it is true that change is the result of prayer, the real purpose of prayer is to bring us into a closer relationship with Almighty God. Prayer would be - and is - a wonderful privilege even if nothing changed. We take our relationship with God in the wrong direction if it depends on whether or not He does what we ask of Him. In reality, our relationship with God is based on whether or not we do what He asks of us!

The first thing we need to know is that our prayers should always be *positive*. We ought to always find something positive to say about the person or the circumstance for which we are praying. We should always remember that God is at work in every person's life in one way or another, and we don't know what God might be doing in their lives. I have said before that we can easily destroy the work of God in a person's life with a simple negative word or attitude. That's why we must take to heart scriptures like "Let your speech be always full of grace, seasoned with salt, so you may know how to answer everyone." (Colossians 4:1) Or, "Do not let any unwholesome talk come out of your mouths, but only what is helpful in building others up according to their needs." (Ephesians 4:29) We should always be positive, and especially in our prayers.

Second, our prayers ought to be *personal*. When interceding for others, we can reflect on how they affect us personally. For instance: when praying for the Philippian church, Paul said; "I have you in my heart...and I long to see you." This was a personal prayer. It reflected his attitude concerning this church. Our prayers can do the same. We may reveal attitudes of love, concern, even anger, guilt, or joy. It is good to reflect our personal feelings toward someone or something. They may bring us joy or make us mad. The circumstance may also bring us joy or make us angry. We need to be honest with God. And, by the way, if you don't know the person or are not personally involved; perhaps you should be! Sometimes just a phone call to let them know you are praying and you wonder if there is anything in particular you should be praying for? It may change a life.

That brings us to the third thing, which is to make it a *purposeful* prayer. I remember my early attempts at prayer; "Bless Mary, bless

Joe, bless Oscar..." It was prayer, and you could say it was even "positive" prayer, but it certainly wasn't personal or purposeful. The point is, if we don't know what we ought to pray...maybe it's an opportunity to find out what to pray for. When I look at the prayers of Paul in his letters, they are always purposeful: (Romans) – I pray that: you might be saved! (Ephesians) – I pray that God may give you the Spirit of wisdom; that your heart may be enlightened; to know Him better; that you may know the hope, the riches, the inheritance, the incomparable power for those who believe; that you may be filled to the measure of all the fullness of God! (Philippians) – I pray that your love may abound in knowledge and insight; that you may be able to discern what is right; that you may be filled with the fruit of righteousness that comes through Jesus Christ! (Colossians) – I pray that God would fill you with the knowledge of His will; that you will live a life worthy of the Lord; that you would bear fruit in every good work; that you may have great endurance and patience! (Thessalonians) – I pray that the Lord make your love increase and overflow for each other; that God would sanctify you through and through; that God may count you worthy of his calling, that He may fulfill every good purpose prompted by your faith! I would like someone to pray these things for me, wouldn't you? Do you see Paul's purposefulness in prayer?

Concerning prayer, A.C. Dixon said; "When we depend upon organizations, we get what organizations can do; when we depend upon education or technology we get what education can do; when we depend upon man, we get what man can do; but when we depend upon prayer, we get what God can do!" We don't pray just because we believe in prayer…We pray because we believe in God!

"Effective Prayer"

Colossians 4:2-6 and 12 – "Devote yourselves to prayer, being watchful and thankful. And pray for us, too, that God may open a door for our message, so that we may proclaim the mystery of Christ, for which I am in chains. Pray that I may proclaim it clearly, as I should. Be wise in the way you act toward outsiders; make the most of every opportunity. Let your conversation be always full of grace, seasoned with salt, so that you may know how to answer everyone.

Epaphras, who is one of you and a servant of Christ Jesus, sends greetings. He is always wrestling in prayer for you, that you may stand firm in all the will of God, mature and fully assured."

I think about how the disciples were with Jesus constantly. They followed Him and witnessed all the things that He said and did. In 2 Peter 1 we read; "We did not follow cleverly invented stories when we told you about the power and the coming of our Lord Jesus Christ, but we were eye witnesses of His majesty." John writes in 1 John 1; "That which was from the beginning, which we have heard, which we have seen with our eyes, which we have looked at and our hands have touched, this we proclaim…" And, in their being with him and observing him, they began to "connect the dots" and realize the importance of Prayer. They soon said in Luke 11:1-4; "Lord, teach us to pray"…Not, teach us how to pray…but teach us to pray.

When we read the accounts of Jesus, we notice that he finds a quiet place to pray; he finds a quiet time to pray; and he has a quiet heart - in that he truly listens for God's voice. Jesus knew, as we must come to know, that prayer is a necessity of life. It is through prayer - talking with and listening to God - that we really come to know Him and create a relationship with Him. It is through prayer that we come to know what God desires for us and from us in this life. Imagine what kind of relationship I would have if I never talked with, or listened to, my wife!

Now, I also have found that just having a quiet time and a quiet place does not necessarily guarantee effectiveness in prayer. I have searched the scriptures and - although there are verses that say things like; "Call unto me and I will give you the desires of your heart" and, "Ask, and it shall be given unto you." Or, "If you believe, you will receive whatever you ask for in prayer." There are also verses like Mark 11:24 - "And when you stand praying, if you hold anything against anyone, forgive him," which is the rest of that verse. Forgiveness is a two way street, regardless of the hurt. If you don't give you don't get. I wonder how many Christians would want God to forgive them in the same way they have forgiven others?

An unforgiving heart will stop our prayers dead in their tracks! Psalm 66:18 is a statement of the obvious; "If I cherish sin in my heart, the Lord will not listen." If there is active sin, or if we are "continuing in sin" as John calls it, our prayers are not even heard. Proverbs 21:13 says; "If a man shuts his ears to the cry of the poor, he too will cry out and not be answered." That simply means that a lack of compassion will hinder our prayers. 1 Peter 3:7 says;

"Husbands, in the same way be considerate as you live with your wives, and treat them with respect as the weaker partner and as heirs with you of the gracious gift of life, so that nothing will hinder your prayers for the eyes of the Lord are on the righteous and his ears are attentive to their prayer". A lack of domestic peace, or a lack of peace in the family, will affect our prayers. 1 John 5:14 says; "This is the confidence we have in approaching God: that if we ask anything *according to his will*, he hears us." Our prayers must be in the will of God. Notice that I did not say "if" it's God's will, but "in" God's will. There are times – for instance – when seeking a job position, when we should pray "If it is God's will"…but most often we already know from His Word if something is God's will. And finally, Matthew 21:22; Mark 11:24; and Romans 14:23 say that faithless prayers are not answered. However, "All things are possible to him who believes"! Why ask God to heal sickness if we don't really believe he can or he will?

So, we are back to unbelief. Jesus said; "O unbelieving generation, how long shall I put up with you?" Perhaps the right thing to do is to be like the father of the demon possessed boy in scripture who cries out; "I do believe, but Lord help me overcome my unbelief!"

In this scripture we have another example we can look at and that is Epaphras. First of all, Paul identifies him as a "servant of Christ". To be a servant, one must have a master. He had made a choice in life, and Christ was his master! Second, it says that Epaphras was "always wrestling in prayer" for them. Another translation says that he "labored" in prayer. Epaphras wasn't a "bless Mary and bless John" kind of person, he was a prayer warrior! He was the type of person described in James 5:16 where it says; "The prayer of a righteous person is powerful and effective!" How we need those who would "labor" in prayer today!

Epaphras was not focused on selfish desires; he was an intercessor, praying for others. As intercessor's we ought to be always praying for the church and its people as well. We surely ought to have a prayer list for the sick and the needy. But, the most important prayer list should be for those whom we know to be unsaved. In the realm of prayer it ought to take precedent because we already know that "It is God's will that not one should perish." Salvation, the forgiveness of sin, and the promise of eternal life is given to every person who repents and receives Christ by faith. I think it is the responsibility of every Christian to pray for the lost. However, we won't pray for the lost unless we have (a.) the right belief and (b.) the right burden.

Do you believe that Jesus meant what he said that a person "must be born again to enter the kingdom of heaven"? We must have the right belief. Do you believe it when Jesus said; "I am the way, the truth, and the life, no man comes to the Father except by me"? Your brother, your sister, your Mother, your Father, your neighbor, your daughter, your son are not good enough to get into heaven! They need Jesus! There are a lot of "good" people headed for Hell! We must have the right belief and the burden or we will not pray!

I read that W.C. Fields was on his deathbed when a friend dropped in to see him and found him reading the Bible. A little surprised, he asked what Fields was doing? "Looking for loopholes, my friend, looking for loopholes." In order to have the right belief, we need to understand that there are no loopholes! God doesn't grade on a curve! Hopefully, if we have the right belief it will give us the right burden. Many hearts have grown cold concerning the eternal destiny of others. We figure they will hear it sooner or later and make their own decision. Or, we may think they have heard and have already made a decision. Is that good enough for you? Not for me either. One of Satan's schemes is to get us to neglect praying for the lost. I looked up the word "intercessor" and one of the meanings was "to represent"…When we pray for others, we are representing them before God. That's what Jesus did on our behalf. He not only came to represent us before God, but to re-present - God to us!

Let me close with this scripture from 2 Corinthians 5 - "Since then, we know what it is to fear the Lord, we try to persuade men…All this is from God, who reconciled himself through Christ and gave us the ministry of reconciliation… We are therefore Christ's ambassadors as though God were making his appeal through us." As Christians it is not only our responsibility to pray; it is our privilege to pray.

2 Timothy 3:16-17 – "All Scripture is God-breathed and is useful for teaching, rebuking, correcting and training in righteousness, so that the servant of God may be thoroughly equipped for every good work."

Paul, in writing to Timothy, shares with him the power of God's Word. You'll read four claims given to us in these two verses:

1. All of it is God's Word.

The Bible is not half inspired and half uninspired. It's not partly fallible, and partly infallible. Now, we all have favorite passages, but it's all His. It is all life-changing. I'll admit there are passages of scripture that I've never preached on. There are passages of scripture that I don't understand; but it's all God's, and it's all God-inspired, and every part of it is there for a purpose.

2. Its instruction is alive and profitable.

The Word is profitable for you and me if we follow and obey it. Get your pen out and in II Timothy 3:16, in that second part of the verse, underline some words. Where he says "*all of it is useful for*" -- here's a word to underline -- "*teaching*." God's Word teaches us, it's good for helping -- underline "*helping*," "*correcting*," and "*training*." It teaches what is right. It corrects us and helps us to get right, stay right, and live right. God's Word is very beneficial, and it's alive.

3. It is comprehensive.

As a pastor, I often asked myself, "How can I meet the needs of everybody here?" And then I realize it's not my job to meet the needs; it's my job to preach the Word. The Word of God is comprehensive. The Holy Spirit bears witness to the Word, Jesus, and he comes and ministers to all the needs today. The Holy Spirit brings us together, and in this time of worship and prayer, he meets our needs. In our walk with God, we have times when God comes especially to do a real, comprehensive work in our lives. These times are literally like the tide; they come and they go according to our need.

4. It can completely equip us for both life and ministry.

God's Word has the ability to come alongside of us and enable us do that which we perhaps could not do ourselves. I learned a long time ago that if you have the Spirit without the Word, you **blow up**; and if you have the Word without the Spirit, you **dry up**. But when you have the Word and the Spirit together, you **grow up**. Sometimes I wonder, when we hold the Word, if we realize what we have in our hand. Sometimes we just kind of take God's Word for granted. The Bible was written over a 1500-year span. It was written by 40 generations, by over 40 authors from every walk of life including kings, peasants, philosophers, fishermen, poets, statesmen, and scholars. It was written in different places, including out in the wilderness, in dungeons, in palaces, inside prison walls, while traveling, on lonely islands, in the midst of war. It was written at different times, sometimes in peace, sometimes in battle. It was written during different moods, some writing from the heights of joy while others wrote from the very depths of sorrow. It was written in three continents: Asia, Africa, and Europe. And it was written in three languages -- Hebrew, Arabic, and Greek. It covered subject matters including hundreds of controversial subjects, yet with harmony and continuity from Genesis to Revelation, there is one unfolding story, and the story is the redemption of man through Jesus Christ.

Ezra 7:10 - "For Ezra had set his heart to study the law of the Lord and to practice it and to teach its statutes and ordinances to Israel."

Voltaire, the French infidel who died in 1778, literally traveled the world, especially "enlightened Europe," speaking against the Word of God. And he predicted that 100 years after his death, the Bible would no longer be on earth. Well, Voltaire died, and 50 years later, the Geneva Bible Society bought his home. Using the presses he had used to produce his atheistic treatises, they have been producing Bibles ever since. "Heaven and earth will pass away, but my Word will never die."

1. Ezra prepared his heart to <u>approach</u> God's Word.

Ezra literally prepared himself in the way that he approached God's Word. He wanted to make sure that he entered into the presence of God's Word in an appropriate manner.

2. Ezra prepared his heart to <u>study</u> God's Word.

As Ezra read it, he allowed his heart to be tender and open to the voice of the Spirit.

3. Ezra prepared to <u>practice</u> what he <u>learned</u>.

Ezra not only read it; but as soon as he read it, he practiced it. He began to apply it to his life.

4. Ezra prepared to share what he learned.

Ezra not only learned it in his own life and practiced and applied it, but he shared it with others, so they could apply it to their lives.

You see, God's Word is powerful. There is something I have learned about the Word of God that I've never forgotten. There are three things you have to do when you come to the Word;

1. Learn It. It can't change you until you know it. "Learn it, and that deals with your head."

2. Love It. You've got to begin to embrace the Word and let it embrace you.

3. Live It. You've got to let the Word of God that comes into your heart go out through your hands,

and you've got to apply it to others.

No wonder the psalmist said, "Your Word I have hid in my heart so that I might not sin against you."

Now what happens is, when we take the Word of God and learn it and love it and live it, we begin to develop biblical convictions. And there are three convictions about the Word of God that I want to make sure that you have today.

First, even when I don't understand it, I'll trust what God said.

Even when I don't understand it, I will take what God has said at face value. I will place my trust not in my understanding, but in God's Word. Naaman did that, remember? Naaman, the captain of the Syrian army, had leprosy, and his little servant girl suggested that he go to her country and see a prophet who could heal him. So off Naaman went to Elijah's house. He arrives in front of the house in his chariot, and Elijah doesn't even come out -- he just sends a servant out. And the servant tells Naaman that the prophet says for him to go down to the Jordan River and dip seven times in it. This ticks Naaman off. In fact, he says, "If I just needed to dip in the water seven times, I could go back to my own swimming pool in Syria. At least, the water's cleaner there." And off he goes. But then remember, his colleagues talk him into going down to the Jordan and dipping seven times, and when he comes out, his flesh is like a newborn baby's.

Now, what's interesting about this is how Naaman responded. He said, "I had thought the prophet would come out and wave his hand, and I would be healed" (he had preconceived how God would answer his prayer. But now, after his healing, he said, "Now I know that there's a God of Israel." Haven't we all done the same thing Naaman did? Haven't we come to God with a prayer request and told him how to answer it? We have this preconceived idea of how he's going to answer it, and we're just ready for it to be step one, two, three, four...No, "even when I don't understand it, I'm going to trust what God has said."

Second, although it seems <u>illogical</u>, I'll <u>obey</u> what God has said.

I will obey what God has said, even if it doesn't make sense. Remember Mary? In John 2, at the wedding in Cana of Galilee? They run out of wine, and Mary looks at the servants, and says, "Whatever he says to you, do it."...And, the Word also tells us not to "lean on our own understanding."

Third, while human opinions vary, God's Word is <u>right</u> on every subject. While human opinions vary, while others will have all sorts of answers, God's Word is right.

One more conviction that'll change your life. I need the Word of God as much as I need food. And when I realize that the Word of God, which is the bread of life, is my spiritual staple that allows me to grow in my walk with him, it begins to change my life. And it begins to build convictions that help me to stand.

God's Word has the power to change your life. I would encourage you not only to read God's Word, and apply it to your heart and life, but also to be very grateful for this precious Word that's been passed onto us.

Matthew 8:1-3 – "When Jesus came down from the mountainside, large crowds followed him. A man with leprosy came and knelt before him and said, "Lord, if you are willing, you can make me clean." Jesus reached out his hand and touched the man. "I am willing," he said. "Be clean!" Immediately he was cleansed of his leprosy."

Luke 7:11-17 – "Soon afterward, Jesus went to a town called Nain, and his disciples and a large crowd went along with him. As he approached the town gate, a dead person was being carried out—the only son of his mother, and she was a widow. And a large crowd from the town was with her. When the Lord saw her, his heart went out to her and he said, "Don't cry." Then he went up and touched the bier they were carrying him on, and the bearers stood still. He said, "Young man, I say to you, get up!" The dead man sat up and began to talk, and Jesus gave him back to his mother. They were all filled with awe and praised God. "A great prophet has appeared among us," they said. "God has come to help his people." This news about Jesus spread throughout Judea and the surrounding country.

Luke 8:40-48 – "Now when Jesus returned, a crowd welcomed him, for they were all expecting him. Then a man named Jairus, a synagogue leader, came and fell at Jesus' feet, pleading with him to come to his house because his only daughter, a girl of about twelve, was dying. As Jesus was on his way, the crowds almost crushed him. And a woman was there who had been subject to bleeding for twelve years, but no one could heal her. She came up behind him and touched the edge of his cloak, and immediately her bleeding stopped. "Who touched me?" Jesus asked. When they all denied it, Peter said, "Master, the people are crowding and pressing against you." But Jesus said, "Someone touched me; I know that power has gone out from me." Then the woman, seeing that she could not go unnoticed, came trembling and fell at his feet. In the presence of all the people, she told why she had touched him and how she had been instantly healed. Then he said to her, "Daughter, your faith has healed you. Go in peace."

We human beings possess five different senses, all of which are important to our existence…as well as to the understanding of the world around us. They are of course, sight, hearing, taste, smell, and touch. Without any one of these we are said to be "handicapped".

It has also been said that if a person were to lose one of these senses, the others would take over and become highly sensitive to make up for the loss. While I would not want to lose any one of my senses, there have been times when I have had a cold and I can't smell anything, and, if it is severe enough, I can't taste anything either.

My eyesight is not what it used to be, and I have to wear reading glasses unless I can change to a larger font. I have suffered some hearing loss, and, as Bill Cosby says; "since turning 50 all the factory warranties have expired and things just start falling apart!"

But, of all our senses, I have never heard of anyone losing their sense of touch. Can you imagine not being able to touch your world? Can you imagine not being able to feel anything? Not being able to touch those you love? We don't think about it much, but touch could be the most sensitive of all our senses. With 1000's of nerve sensors sending impulses to the brain, we touch things all the time, everyday, and don't really think about it.

There are times when we deliberately touch something to see how it feels texture wise. Or, in the case of a grandchild, we touch because we desire intimate contact. Touch certainly stirs within us certain emotions like love, and compassion. Sometimes our touch can even effect change in that which we touch; (a pool of quiet water is affected by our touch,) A touch can be creative and sensitive, or it can be destructive. It can be a caress, or it can be a destructive blow! Let's look at the power of touch as it concerns Christ...

During times of prayer, I have heard the words; "Lord, touch his life"... Now, this could mean anything from a "smack him along side the head!" to "Give him a holy hug!" Or, touch his hurt and make him well. But, I believe those simple words have more power than we think. When we pray these words, it may be for one of two reasons; (1.) We don't know exactly what we specifically should pray for, so we simply pray for God to "touch" them. Or (2.) Because we really understand the power that is released and received in a touch, and especially the touch of God. In fact, we could say these words in prayer for both reasons.

The touch of God is a powerful touch. It is an intimate touch. It is a transforming touch. The touch of God always invokes change, and, it is always needed change in the object of His touch. We know there is something that needs to be changed, so we pray; "Lord, touch... It may be a healing touch; it may be a spiritual touch; a comforting touch; a change in circumstance touch; or even change of thinking or action or lifestyle touch; but it is a powerful touch we are asking for!

It transforms those with sickness. In Matthew 8:14 it says that "When Jesus came into Peter's house, he saw Peter's Mother-in-law lying in bed with a fever". He "touched" her and the fever left and she got up and served him. There is healing power in the touch of God.

It transforms the deaf. In Mark 7:31-35 it says; "Then Jesus left the vicinity of Tyre and went through Sidon, down to the sea of Galilee and into the region of the Decapolis. There some people brought to him a man who was deaf, and could hardly talk, and they begged Jesus to 'place his hand on the man'. After he took him aside, away from the crowd, Jesus put his fingers into the man's ears. Then he spat on his finger and touched the man's tongue. He looked up to heaven and with a deep sigh said "Eph-pha-tha" which means "be opened" At this, the man's ears were opened, and his tongue was loosed, and he began to speak plainly,"

It transforms the blind. Matthew 9:27-30 "As Jesus went out from there, two blind men followed him calling out; "Have mercy on us Son of David." When he had gone indoors, the blind men came to him, and he asked them; "Do you believe I am able to do this?" "Yes, Lord" they replied. Then he 'touched' their eyes and said; "According to your faith will it be done to you"; and their sight was restored". There is another instance when Jesus put mud on a man's eyes and with that touch, he was able to see.

It transforms the doomed. In Matthew 8:1-3 it says; "When he came down from the mountain side, a large crowd followed him. A man with leprosy came and knelt before him and said; "Lord, if you are willing, you can make me clean". Jesus reached out his hand and 'touched' the man. "I am willing" he said, "Be clean" and immediately he was cured of his leprosy. This man was doomed to live out his life alone, with painful skin lesions, and with no one able to 'touch' him. Doomed to never again feel the touch of a loved one. Yet, he was 'touched' by Jesus, and his life was transformed.

It transforms the dead. Luke 8:49-55 - "While Jesus was still speaking, someone came from the house of Jarius; "Your daughter is dead" he said, "Don't bother the master any more". Jesus said to Jarius; "Don't be afraid, just believe, and she will be healed." When he arrived at the house of Jarius, the people were weeping and wailing and mourning for her. "Stop wailing" Jesus said. "She is not dead but asleep." They laughed at him, knowing that she was dead. But Jesus 'touched' her, took her by the hand and said; "My child, get up!" (Now, I want you to carefully notice what it says next) "<u>Her spirit returned</u>, and at once she stood up." I don't have time to go into that, but just chew on it a little! "Her spirit returned"... Hmmm.

It transforms the dismayed and fearful. Matthew 17:1-7 "After six days, Jesus took with him Peter, James, and John the brother of James, and led them up a high mountain by themselves. There he was transfigured before them. His face shone like the sun, his clothes became white as the light. Just then there appeared before them Moses and Elijah, talking with Jesus. Peter said to Jesus, "Lord, it is good for us to be here. If you wish, I will put up three shelters...one for you, one for Moses, and one for Elijah"...While he was still speaking, a bright cloud enveloped them, and a voice from the cloud said; "This is my Son, whom I love; with Him I am well pleased. Listen to Him!"... When the disciples heard this, they fell facedown to the ground, terrified! But Jesus came and "touched" them saying "Don't be afraid". Let me just encourage you this morning, that if you are dismayed or fearful...look up all the "fear not's" in the Bible and take to heart the promises given for each one.

Finally, there are times when we may need to be "touched" twice. In Mark 8:22-25 we have another story of a blind man. It says; "They came to Bethsaida, and some people brought a blind man and begged Jesus to touch him. (Here is another thing to pay attention to); Do you know how many times it says that someone brought a person in need to Jesus? That ought to speak to us about our friends and family and neighbors. "When he had spit on the man's eyes and touched him, Jesus asked; "Do you see anything?" He looked up and said, "I see people; they look like trees walking around" (In other words, his vision was blurred) "Once more Jesus touched the man's eyes. Then his eyes were opened, his sight was restored, and he saw everything clearly."

Now, here's what you can take from all of this; There are those on our prayer lists who are not only physically sick, but spiritually sick. They have sin-fever and a spiritual temperature of 110* They need the touch of God in their life. There are those who are deaf to God's Word. Their hearts are so hardened they cannot hear the truth, and they need the touch of God. There are those who are spiritually blind. The Bible says in 2 Corinthians 4:4 that "the god of this age has blinded their minds" not their eyes, but their minds, "so they cannot see the light of the gospel" and they live in darkness! They need the touch of God on their lives. There are those who are doomed. Doomed to an eternal life in the "lake of fire" of hell, eternally separated from God, unless someone brings them to Jesus!

They need Him to touch their lives and bring the assurance of eternal life that salvation brings; and a transformation in their lives.

Ephesians 2:1 tells us that before coming to Christ, we were "dead in our transgressions and sins." This is the situation of everyone who is lost and without God; spiritually dead, and facing what the Bible calls "the second death". We need to pray for God to touch them with his life-giving Spirit! The touch of God is a powerful touch, it is a transforming touch, it is an intimate touch, it is a healing touch, and it is a saving touch! For whom will you pray for God to "touch" today?

James 1:19-25 – "My dear brothers and sisters, take note of this: Everyone should be quick to listen, slow to speak and slow to become angry, because human anger does not produce the righteousness that God desires. Therefore, get rid of all moral filth and the evil that is so prevalent and humbly accept the word planted in you, which can save you. Do not merely listen to the word, and so deceive yourselves. Do what it says. Anyone who listens to the word but does not do what it says is like someone who looks at his face in a mirror and, after looking at himself, goes away and immediately forgets what he looks like. But whoever looks intently into the perfect law that gives freedom, and continues in it—not forgetting what they have heard, but doing it—they will be blessed in what they do.

The Book of James is written in a very direct way. It contains a lot of "imperatives" or things that we <u>must</u> do because of our faith. The Book of John 20:31 states "These things are written that you may believe…" But, the Book of James is written to give us the things we need to DO because of what we believe. I would say that most of Paul's writings were for the same reason.

I want to focus in on the words in verse 19 - "Quick to listen" and bring out four principles of faith that concern how and why we should listen to God's Word. How we hear has a direct effect on our faith;

Romans 10:17 – "Consequently, faith comes from hearing the message, and the message is heard through the word about Christ."

John 10:27 - Jesus said "My sheep listen to my voice; I know them and they follow me."

Our readiness to hear reflects upon our relationship with God. For instance; There are those who are "slow to hear." These listeners can hear sermon after sermon and it never seems to affect their lives or their thinking. They may even nod their heads in agreement at some point, or even understand that what they heard was truth, but it makes no difference at all. Matthew 13:13-15 – ""Though seeing, they do not see; though hearing, they do not hear or understand. In them is fulfilled the prophecy of Isaiah: 'You will be ever hearing but never understanding; you will be ever seeing but never perceiving. For this people's heart has become calloused; they hardly hear with their ears, and they have closed their eyes. Otherwise they might see with their eyes, hear with their ears, understand with their hearts and turn, and I would heal them."

Then there are those who have "selective hearing". They only hear what they want to hear. They "tune out" the things they don't want or don't like to hear. Sometimes we have selective hearing on a subconscious level. A mother, for instance can hear her child whimper while she is in the midst of a sound sleep.

There's a story told of the old Indian who was walking with a friend down the busy and noisy streets of New York. He suddenly stopped and said; "Did you hear that?" "Hear what?" "Did you hear that cricket?" "How can you hear a cricket in the midst of all this noise?" The old Indian bent over a potted tree on the curb, and sure enough, there was a cricket. "It all depends on what you are listening for" he said.

Then, of course, there are the good listeners. They are the seekers.

They are seeking to know and seeking to grow. This is the kind of listener Cornelius was in Acts 10:30 -33 – "Three days ago I was in my house praying at this hour, at three in the afternoon. Suddenly a man in shining clothes stood before me and said, 'Cornelius, God has heard your prayer and remembered your gifts to the poor. Send to Joppa for Simon who is called Peter. He is a guest in the home of Simon the tanner, who lives by the sea.' So I sent for you immediately, and it was good of you to come. Now we are all here in the presence of God to listen to everything the Lord has commanded you to tell us." Good listeners are always ready to hear God speak. They are eager to take notes and hungry to learn. They are literally seeking to grow spiritually and not just content to let spiritual growth just happen to them. There is a certain part or parts of spiritual growth that will happen or "rub off" just because we are there! However, this type of listener desires life change!

Verse 21 of our scripture in James says – "Therefore, get rid of all moral filth and the evil that is so prevalent and humbly accept the word planted in you, which can save you. Do not merely listen to the word, and so deceive yourselves. Do what it says." Remember, James is speaking to Christians. It would seem to indicate there were sins still left over from their past. Sometimes our repentance, our severance with the past, is not as complete as it should be. And, as long as sin is left to linger in our lives, our faith will never really flourish like God desires. Paul says the same thing when he admonishes us to "Put off the old self, and put on the new self."

Verse 21 b. "Humbly accept the word *planted* in you." If the

Word of God is only on the surface, it will never have the kind of influence it is meant to have. It has to be firmly planted! The Parable of the Sower gives us a picture of that surface Christianity; when the Word is only on the surface, is soon stolen by Satan, scorched, or blown away. But, when it is planted in good soil; "it produces a crop yielding a hundred, sixty, or thirty times what was sown."

Finally, he says in verse 22 that we can't just listen to the Word, we must be do'ers of the Word. We may hear the Word, and even have the Word in our hearts, but if we never apply it, we never really grow. Many Christians wonder why nothing seems to be happening in their lives when it comes to God, when they themselves are the holdup. These are the principles that James says we must DO in order for our faith to grow and flourish and produce fruit.

James - 1:26 - 2:6 – "Those who consider themselves religious and yet do not keep a tight rein on their tongues deceive themselves, and their religion is worthless. Religion that God our Father accepts as pure and faultless is this: to look after orphans and widows in their distress and to keep oneself from being polluted by the world. My brothers and sisters, believers in our glorious Lord Jesus Christ must not show favoritism. Suppose a man comes into your meeting wearing a gold ring and fine clothes, and a poor man in filthy old clothes also comes in. If you show special attention to the man wearing fine clothes and say, "Here's a good seat for you," but say to the poor man, "You stand there" or "Sit on the floor by my feet," have you not discriminated among yourselves and become judges with evil thoughts? Listen, my dear brothers and sisters: Has not God chosen those who are poor in the eyes of the world to be rich in faith and to inherit the kingdom he promised those who love him? But you have dishonored the poor. Is it not the rich who are exploiting you? Are they not the ones who are dragging you into court?"

Shortly after the close of the Civil War, a former slave entered a fashionable church in Richmond, one Sunday morning at the beginning of a communion service. When the time came, he walked down the aisle and knelt at the altar. A rustle of shock and anger swept through the congregation. A distinguished layman immediately stood up, stepped forward to the altar and knelt beside this Christian brother. Captured by his spirit, the congregation followed. The layman who set the example: Robert E. Lee. Now there's a monument I would like to see, Lee and an ex-slave kneeling in prayer at the altar of Christ.

When anyone walks into a church they must feel like the only one who is getting honored is Jesus Christ and no matter what background that person is from they will respect the fact that God is center focus in his church and not people. Not the pastor. Not the leadership. James is instructing the church on how to do visitor and greeter ministry. As a body of believers Jesus does not want the warmth or honor of our welcome to be determined by the status or apparent wealth of the visitor. James is obviously forbidding a practice already in progress. Only accepting certain people will not make a full church but a building that is not a church at all. If we are a partial disciple in a partial Church then it is true that we serve only a partial God. Being impartial is one of God's attributes.

(1) Deut 10:17 "For the LORD your God is God of gods and Lord of lords, the great God, mighty and awesome, who shows no partiality nor takes a bribe."

(2) Acts 10:34 Then Peter opened his mouth and said: "In truth I perceive that God shows no partiality."

(3) Rom 2:11 "For there is no partiality with God."

(4) Gal 2:6 "But from those who seemed to be something whatever they were, it makes no difference to me; God shows personal favoritism to no man for those who seemed to be something added nothing to me."

(5) Eph 6:9 "And you, masters, do the same things to them, giving up threatening, knowing that your own Master also is in heaven, and there is no partiality with Him."

(6) Col 3:25 "But he who does wrong will be repaid for what he has

done, and there is no partiality." It is an attitude of Jesus' –

Matthew 22:16 "They sent their disciples to him along with the Herodians. "Teacher," they said, "we know that you are a man of integrity and that you teach the way of God in accordance with the truth. You aren't swayed by others, because you pay no attention to who they are." Don't favor gorgeous over homely, thin over plump, well dressed over barely dressed, tattoo's or pierced should not matter…and, church is not a singles bar…church is a good place to find a husband or wife, but don't come for that reason. Don't favor one color over the other, don't favor clean over dirty; and do not favor finances or social standing. Those are some ways we show favoritism and there are others.

James says in verse 4 that when we show favoritism we become judges with evil thoughts. Our evil intentions are at work and we are looking for personal gain. It is evil for a Pastor who does not preach repentance or confront sin because he is afraid he will lose a big giver or does not want to offend!

James is showing us that when people come into the house of God knowing that they can get attention because of who they are and what they have, it is going to rob the house of God from being what it should be; a great equalizer.

A comparable today would be how we would react to the President of the U. S. A. and a homeless person coming to our assembly.

Church - It's not a place to worship people, but to worship the Almighty God… Not a place to look at each other, but to fix our eyes on Jesus… Not a place for pride or prejudice. Luke 18:9-14 –

"To some who were confident of their own righteousness and looked down on everyone else, Jesus told this parable: "Two men went up to the temple to pray, one a Pharisee and the other a tax collector. The Pharisee stood by himself and prayed: 'God, I thank you that I am not like other people—robbers, evildoers, adulterers—or even like this tax collector. I fast twice a week and give a tenth of all I get.' "But the tax collector stood at a distance. He would not even look up to heaven, but beat his breast and said, 'God, have mercy on me, a sinner.' "I tell you that this man, rather than the other, went home justified before God. For all those who exalt themselves will be humbled, and those who humble themselves will be exalted."

"Two Gifts of God"

I want to tell you today about two gifts from Almighty God that you can receive and take with you that can change your life forever! This book, that we call the Bible or the Word of God or the Scriptures, is truly the inspired words of our Sovereign God, the Creator of heaven and earth, who inspired the hearts and minds of those who wrote down everything God desired to have written in His Word. I have read this Word, and I find that in it is revealed the fact that all mankind has two basic problems; One is that we have sinned – Romans 3:23 says; "All have sinned and come short of the glory of God." – Romans 5:12; "Therefore, just as sin entered the world through one man, and death through sin, in this way death came to all men because all have sinned"! However, it also says that we have a gift, which is the grace of God given through Jesus Christ His Son. A gift that brings forgiveness of sin through His final sacrifice on the Cross for all who believe! "For the wages of sin is death, but the gift of God is eternal life in Christ Jesus our Lord". This is God's gift of salvation - by His grace - through Jesus - for man's first problem of sin.

Our second problem is that we are sinners! The Book of Galatians chapter 5 speaks of our "sinful nature" – "So, I say, live by the Spirit, and you will not gratify the desires of the sinful nature. For the sinful nature does what is contrary to the Spirit. They are in conflict with each other so you do not do what you want." Even if we have believed and accepted God's first gift of salvation in Christ, we still have within us a sinful nature. A nature that desires all of the self-seeking things that lead to destruction (Sexual immorality, lust, impure things, idolatry, hatred, rage, jealousy, drunkenness, selfishness) "Those who live like this will not inherit the kingdom of God" it says.

So, to help us overcome this battle of our sinful nature, God has given us a second gift; the gift of the Holy Spirit. Before ascending into heaven, in the Book of Acts 1:4, Jesus himself said to His disciples; "Do not leave Jerusalem but wait for the gift my Father promised, which you have heard me speak about"…This was God's gift of the Holy Spirit.

According to the Bible, the Holy Spirit;

1. "convicts" (of guilt in regard to sin) - John 16:8
2. "guides" (into all truth) - John 16:13
3. "reveals" (God and the wisdom of God) - 1Corinthians 2:10
4. "comforts" …
5. "empowers"
6. "gives gifts" - 1Corinthians 12
7. "bears fruit" - Galatians 5:22

All of these things give us the power we need to live the Christian life He has called us to live.

In his book on the Holy Spirit, Billy Graham says that we are given a two-fold gift from God. First is "the work of Jesus, the Son of God, for us; and second, the work of the Holy Spirit in us. One is our *eternal* gift and the other is our *internal* gift." Both are intricate parts of our growth as Christians.

In His Word, God gives us four things that become a part of our lives when we accept God's second gift;

1. Being led by the Spirit.
2. Having the power of the Spirit.
3. Bearing the "fruit" of the Spirit.
4. Using the "gifts" of the Spirit.

The Holy Spirit's primary goal is to "lead" us into Christlikeness; holiness; and righteousness. There is a difference between being "directed" and being "led" - as in someone giving directions or leading you themselves.

Someone has once said that "knowledge is power". I think the power of the Holy Spirit comes from the knowledge of who He is and what He does. The Bible says; "The things of God are foolishness to those who are without the Spirit." Our knowledge of the Holy Spirit gives us power to overcome our sinful nature; power to overcome the temptations of Satan in our lives; power to live Christlike and holy lives; as we grow in our knowledge of Him; The power we need to - "witness" (To witness as to our *faith* and that which we have *experienced!*) Also the power to stand; power to change; power to grow; power to apply that which we have been given - our gifts and talents - and power to obey that which we have learned and understood.

God's second gift of the Holy Spirit also helps us to bear the fruit of the Spirit. What is the fruit? - It is found in (Galatians 5:22) –

"love, joy, peace, patience, kindness, goodness, faithfulness, gentleness, and self-control". To understand the Spirit's role in the bearing of fruit, we need to turn to John 15:1-8 – "I am the true vine, and my Father is the gardener. He cuts off every branch in me that bears no fruit, while every branch that does bear fruit he prunes so that it will be even more fruitful. You are already clean because of the word I have spoken to you. Remain in me, as I also remain in you. No branch can bear fruit by itself; it must remain in the vine. Neither can you bear fruit unless you remain in me. "I am the vine; you are the branches. If you remain in me and I in you, you will bear much fruit; apart from me you can do nothing. If you do not remain in me, you are like a branch that is thrown away and withers; such branches are picked up, thrown into the fire and burned. If you remain in me and my words remain in you, ask whatever you wish, and it will be done for you. This is to my Father's glory, that you bear much fruit, showing yourselves to be my disciples."

The proof of God's presence in our life is not "gifts" it is "fruit"! If Jesus is the Vine and we are the branches, the Holy Spirit is the "sap" that flows and brings "life" to the branches. Spiritual fruit is just like real fruit, it first appears as a tiny bud… it soon becomes a flower… and then a small fruit appears and begins to grow into a full blown fruit! This fruit has within it the potential to produce more fruit! I don't, at this time, want to get into the individual fruit of the Spirit, as much as gain an understanding of the role of the Spirit in our Christian walk. Again, we humans have two problems; the fact that we have sinned, and the fact that we are sinners. God, in His love and mercy has dealt with both. For the first he has given us His Son; for the second, He has given us His Spirit.

1Corinthians 12:7 tells us that the gifts are given "for the common good." God has gifted us to help us function effectively as Christians; as His Church; and to prepare us to be participators in rather than spectators of, God's work in the world. 1Peter 4:10 says; "Each one should use whatever gift he has received to serve others, faithfully administering God's grace in its various forms." We use our gifts and talents to serve one another and the church for God's glory. Whatever gifts or talents we are blessed with we are to use for the common good of the church; first, to promote growth and second, to bring unity. God's purpose is not to bring *competition* but *contribution*!

John 21:1-17 – "Afterward Jesus appeared again to his disciples, by the Sea of Galilee. It happened this way: Simon Peter, Thomas (also known as Didymus), Nathanael from Cana in Galilee, the sons of Zebedee, and two other disciples were together. "I'm going out to fish," Simon Peter told them, and they said, "We'll go with you." So they went out and got into the boat, but that night they caught nothing. Early in the morning, Jesus stood on the shore, but the disciples did not realize that it was Jesus. He called out to them, "Friends, haven't you any fish?" "No," they answered. He said, "Throw your net on the right side of the boat and you will find some." When they did, they were unable to haul the net in because of the large number of fish.

Then the disciple whom Jesus loved said to Peter, "It is the Lord!" As soon as Simon Peter heard him say, "It is the Lord," he wrapped his outer garment around him (for he had taken it off) and jumped into the water. The other disciples followed in the boat, towing the net full of fish, for they were not far from shore, about a hundred yards. When they landed, they saw a fire of burning coals there with fish on it, and some bread. Jesus said to them, "Bring some of the fish you have just caught." So Simon Peter climbed back into the boat and dragged the net ashore. It was full of large fish, 153, but even with so many the net was not torn. Jesus said to them, "Come and have breakfast." None of the disciples dared ask him, "Who are you?" They knew it was the Lord. Jesus came, took the bread and gave it to them, and did the same with the fish. This was now the third time Jesus appeared to his disciples after he was raised from the dead.

When they had finished eating, Jesus said to Simon Peter, "Simon son of John, do you love me more than these?" "Yes, Lord," he said, "you know that I love you." Jesus said, "Feed my lambs." Again Jesus said, "Simon son of John, do you love me?" He answered, "Yes, Lord, you know that I love you." Jesus said, "Take care of my sheep." The third time he said to him, "Simon son of John, do you love me?" Peter was hurt because Jesus asked him the third time, "Do you love me?" He said, "Lord, you know all things; you know that I love you." Jesus said, "Feed my sheep."

His name is Simon Peter. We remember him as the disciple who tried to walk on water, but started sinking when the wind and the waves blew his faith away. He was the one who testified Jesus as the Son of God, yet denied him three times in one night. He swore never to forsake his master, but ran away for fear of his life. Simon Peter, a man of broken promises…a man of failure.

His name is Simon Peter. We remember him as a great Apostle. He boldly and tirelessly proclaimed Jesus as the Son of God. He baptized hundreds and perhaps thousands of people. He performed many miracles by healing the sick and even raising the dead. People chased his shadow believing that if his shadow fell upon them, they would be healed. Simon Peter: a man of great success and fame in the church of Jesus Christ.

What made the difference between the first Simon Peter, and the second Simon Peter was the account in our scripture of Jesus – as he walked - approaching the shoreline – He was the God of "Second Chances".

It is interesting that in Mark's gospel, we read about the women going to the tomb to anoint the body of Jesus; there they see an angel who tells them "Don't be alarmed, you are looking for Jesus the Nazarene, who was crucified. He has risen! He is not here. See the place where they laid him. But, go tell his disciples *AND PETER*, he is going ahead of you into Galilee." This kind of gives us a little hint that Jesus was especially concerned for Peter; "make sure you tell Peter!"

The same reference in the Gospel of Luke says that two angels appeared and said "Why do you look for the living among the dead? He is not here! He has risen!" It goes on to say that when they came back from the tomb they told all this to the disciples, but they "did not believe the women, because their words seemed to them like nonsense. *Peter, however*, got up and ran to the tomb; he saw the strips of linen and went away wondering to himself what had happened." John's account, of course, tells us that both he and Peter ran to the tomb...The curious thing about John's Gospel is that the verses previous to our text – John 20:30 seemed to be the end of the story. It's like John recounts the appearances of Jesus – but leaves out the Great Commission and the Ascension; and says "Jesus did many other miraculous signs in the presence of his disciples, which are not recorded in this book. But these things are written that you may believe that Jesus is the Christ, the Son of God, and that by believing you may have life in his name...The end.

Then, chapter 21 is like an after-thought; "Oh yea, I almost forgot the time Jesus appeared on the shore when we were fishing..." John was there, and gives us the account of Jesus reinstating Peter; giving Peter a second chance.

It is interesting that the first time Jesus called Peter he was also fishing. In Luke 5:5 Jesus tells Peter to "go out into deeper water and let down your nets for a catch." Peter says, "Master, we have worked all night and haven't caught a thing!" In John 21 it says that they again fished all night and caught nothing, then Jesus comes and says "Let down your nets on the right side of the boat and you will find some fish." In Luke 5 they caught so many fish their nets began to break. In John 21 "they were unable to haul in the net for the large number of fish." In the first encounter, Jesus was in the boat with them; this time they were on their own. However, Jesus was near, and directed them - there is significance in that.

At any rate, John thinks this is too much like dejavu' and shouts "It's the Lord!"... and of course, Peter jumps out of the boat!

Now, all that being said, how do you suppose Peter felt? He had fled at the first sign of trouble; He denied even knowing Jesus for fear of his own life; He didn't believe the women, nor did he believe the two men from Emmaus! He felt defeated, and now, here was Jesus - just like the first time they had met. But, what would he say? Could he still love me after all I have done? Is there still a place and a purpose for me in his kingdom? Will he give me another chance?

We soon find out that it was not Jesus intent to push the knife of guilt any deeper into Peter's heart, but rather it was his intention to remove Peter's guilt; to remove the heart ache; and offer Peter a chance to start over. So, in full view of all the other disciples that were there, Jesus turns to Peter and says, "Peter, do you love me more than these?" (Which could be a reference to "more than the other disciples", or "more than fishing") Jesus deliberately uses "Agape'" as the form of the word love; And, Peter says "Yes, Lord, you know that I love you." Peter's form of the word however is "Philio" which means "friend"; "Lord, you are my best friend!" Jesus tells him "Good, here's the priority – "Feed my sheep!" Again Jesus says; "Simon, do you love – (Agape') me?" Peter again uses the word "Philio" - "Lord, you know that I really care about you."

And, Jesus says "Here's the priority – Take care of my sheep!" The third time Jesus asks the same question using the same form "Agape" This time Peter answers "Lord, you know all things, and you know that I "Agape" you" - I love you with a divine love, a godly love! Jesus again says, "Here's the priority, Feed my sheep!"

When Jesus first met Peter in Matthew 4:19 he said "Come follow me, and I will make you fishers of men"…now, once again, forgiven and reinstated, Jesus says to Peter "Follow me!"

There are two other separate occasions when Jesus appeared to His disciples, yet Jesus did not confront Peter. He gave him time! Then he gave him a second chance. Instead of rebuking Peter for his failures, Jesus gives him another chance to prove himself. Jesus was not looking to Peter's past, he was looking to Peter's future! He was looking to what Peter was going to do from that moment on.

Now, all of this of course begs the question; How many of us find ourselves in a position spiritually, in our relationship with Christ and our service to the kingdom where we could use a second chance? A second chance to tell Jesus, the risen, living Lord, that we love him, and we want to prove it by "feeding his sheep" and "fishing for men." We want to serve him in whatever capacity he desires to use us. By the way, just so I'm clear, we only get second chances in this life. Now is the time!

Proverbs 11:24-25 – "One person gives freely, yet gains even more; another withholds unduly, but comes to poverty. A generous person will prosper; whoever refreshes others will be refreshed.

Back in the Book of Genesis 12:2-3 God promised Abraham a blessing so powerful that it would impact all the nations of the earth. God also said that through Abraham and his seed, all the nations of the earth would be blessed. (It is interesting to note that in Galatians 3:16 Christ is referred to as the "seed of Abraham") So, through Abraham, and ultimately through Christ, the blessings of God would flow out to all the world; especially and ultimately the blessing of salvation.

God's Word has a lot to say about the blessings of God. The power of God's blessing can be a transforming power that is to flow through the life of a believer in many different dimensions. According to Acts 3:26 – the blessings of God are intended to turn people's hearts from sinful ways and turn them back to God. We could say that the central purpose of God's many blessings are to show him to the world, and turn their hearts back to him.

Along with our scripture text from Proverbs 11, there are some other associated blessings I don't want you to miss out on:

First, Malachi 3:10 – "Bring the whole tithe into the storehouse, that there may be food in my house. Test me in this," says the LORD Almighty, "and see if I will not throw open the floodgates of heaven and pour out so much blessing that you will not have room enough for it." While this is not necessarily a message on tithing, I have come to know that God certainly blesses us when we let his financial blessings flow through us.

Here is another from Luke 6:38 – "Give, and it will be given to you. A good measure, pressed down, shaken together and running over, will be poured into your lap. For with the measure you use, it will be measured to you." I've chosen to sum up that principle this morning by taking some liberty with the Morton Salt slogan "When it rains, it pours", and changing it to "When He reigns, it pours."

Flip Wilson was a popular comedian several years ago, some of you are old enough to remember him, but one of his characters was a Preacher at the "What's Happening Now Church." In a skit that he did He'd yell: "If this church is going to serve god it's got to get down on its knees and crawl!!!" And the congregation would yell back "Make it crawl preacher, make it crawl! And then he would yell: "And once this church has learned to crawl, it's got to get up on its feet and walk!!!" And the congregation would yell back "Make it walk preacher, make it walk." Then he would say: "Once this church has learned to walk it's got begin to learn to run!!!" And they would yell, "Make it run, preacher, make it run!" Then he would say, "And in order to run, its got reach deep down into pockets and learn to give!!!" And after a pause, the people would say "Make it crawl preacher, make it crawl!"

The blessing of God is not intended to make us materially rich. In fact, material things have a way of hindering God's blessing! While he has promised to provide our needs, our hearts must be set on Him and His Kingdom; "Seek Ye first the kingdom of God and His righteousness, and all these things will be added unto you."

I could mention many ways in which we feel blessed by God; and they all are true blessings, but I think one of the most important and fulfilling dimensions of God's blessings is when we allow ourselves to become "channels" of God's blessing. The blessings of God in our lives, whatever we have received from God in our lives, be it financial, good relationships, love, grace, or peace, they must flow through us to reach people and show them God. When we are channels of those blessings, God will turn their hearts toward Him. When we think of the many ways we have been blessed, we ought to ask ourselves if we have just received those blessings and held on to them for ourselves, or have we had opportunity to be a "channel" and shared that blessing with someone in need?

I want to give you just five quick areas of our lives where I feel we can all become greater channels of blessing: I believe that God can take these areas and pour out so much blessing upon them that they will have an impact on our families, our community, and even our world, in a powerful way that has eternal results.

The first area that we don't usually think of as a blessing is prayer. We never think of saying "I feel blessed today because I can be a channel of God's blessing on those for whom I am praying." The power of prayer is incredible! If we could see the blessings that are unleashed through prayer, we would all become prayer warriors! The next time you pray for someone, don't just ask God to fill their need;

ask God to release his blessings upon them, that they might turn to Him.

Second, God wants us to be channels of Love. We receive God's unconditional love, through Jesus Christ, we ought to let the love of God flow through us. The Word says that "we love because He first loved us." Because God is love, he certainly has an infinite supply to pour into us so we can pour into others. I have said this before and it bears repeating; "If you are not going to love people – all people – unconditionally…then don't tell them God does!" It's the most negative form of evangelism there is.

Third, what about being a channel of God's forgiveness? We ought to say that "I feel blessed today because I am forgiven! I have received God's undeserved forgiveness." It's called Grace. The Lord, in fact, commands us to forgive others with the same kind of forgiveness we have received, and, He says, if we don't forgive others then he won't forgive us; that's a sobering thought. Forgiveness is a blessing that **must** be passed on.

Forth, just as God's Word is a blessing to our lives, so our words can be a blessing in the lives of others. We can never underestimate the power of words. Words can bless, encourage, help, lift up and build up, but they can also have the opposite effect. Think about the fact that the hearts of people can be turned toward God because of our words; they can also be turn away because of our words. If we want to be channels of God's blessing, we must choose our words wisely and carefully.

Finally, of course, we can be channels of all the blessings God has given us through our actions and deeds. Using our talents, gifts, time, resources, or whatever we have, to be channels of blessing to people in need. In the Church Doxology we sing "Praise God from whom all blessings flow"...Do we really believe that? I have to ask myself – "Am I living that?"

Our scripture says "He who refreshes others will himself be refreshed." We have often heard that we are God's hands and feet, we are God's eyes and ears and God's heart to the world... As we bless those around us, God pours his blessings back in an abundant supply. Proverbs 28:20 says "A faithful man will abound with blessings."

Captain Levy, a believer from Philadelphia, was once asked how he could give so much to the Lord's work and still possess great wealth. The Captain replied, "Oh, as I shovel it out, He shovels it in, and the Lord has a bigger shovel."

You can't put a price tag on the satisfaction you get when you make someone's life a little bit better. So, if you really feel blessed this morning – Pass it on!

There were two seas that dominated the land of Jesus, the land where he was born and grew up, the land in which he lived and ministered, the land which some today call Israel, and others call Palestine. One of these two great bodies of water, filled with fresh water, fed by the head-waters of the Jordan River at Caesarea Philippi, was the center of much of Jesus' activity during his ministry. It was a scene of sometimes tranquil, sometimes fierce beauty; for the length of its almost thirteen miles, fish abound in its waters, both in numbers and in kinds. As a result, from before the time of Christ to the present day, the boats of fishermen have dotted its surface and shoreline, giving birth to cities, like Capernaum and Bethsaida, that were haven and home to Jesus and his closest disciples…the fishermen; Peter, James and John. It is encircled by pebbled shores and rolling green slopes; trees huddle along its shores and sink their roots deep into the refreshment at water's edge; the surrounding countryside is a patchwork of teeming cities and valuable farmland. At the southern tip of this sea, the Jordan River, having passed through the Sea of Galilee, continues its southerly trek through the land in which Jesus lived. Seventy miles south, after winding like a snake through the countryside, the Jordan empties into the other sea. This second sea Jesus knew, boasted none of the characteristics of its northern counterpart. It receives water every day from the Jordan River, water that has collected mineral substances from the soil of the area, such as the chlorides of sodium, magnesium, and calcium. There these substances stay, for unlike the Sea of Galilee to the north, this sea has no outlet; it receives but does not give. As a result, the water there is about four times as salty as the ocean. The water is bitter to the taste and undrinkable. In this southern sea can be found barely a trace of life; no fish, not even shellfish or coral are found beneath its surface. The landscape all around is unoccupied, it is a desert: a dry, rocky, wilderness. The dry, burnt look of the shoreline, the sometimes over-powering heat of the region, the lingering stench of sulfur, the apparent lack of life in and around the sea all combine to make its name—"The Dead

Sea"— a fitting description.

I mention these two seas as a parable: one is a scene of beauty, a center of commerce, whose shores and depths teem with life; the other is quite the opposite; its shores are barren, the atmosphere is harsh, and its bitter waters cannot sustain life nor quench thirst. The Sea of Galilee is a blessing...the Dead Sea is not.

In my last message, I spoke of the blessing of God to Abraham: "I will make you a blessing, and all nations shall be blessed through you." I spoke also of the various ways and dimensions through which God chooses to bless, and when we think of blessings, we always seem to equate it with prosperity. However, the blessings of God go far beyond monetary and material things to the real reason and purpose for God's blessing...and that is to turn people's hearts toward Him. So it is that God's plan has always been that through Abraham, through Christ His Son, and through you and I – the church – the blessings of God would flow out to the entire world. The key word being "through" we are to be channels of God's blessings in whatever form they may take; in whatever capacity He gives us.

The list of examples is endless, but let's thinks about the most obvious; If we are blessed with wealth, we can use it to buy whatever we need, want, or desire, and we even store up things we don't need and don't use. Or, we can be channels of God's blessing and use it to help others find and know God and the truth of the Gospel. We can use it to support missions and missionaries all over the world. We can use it to support and keep our local church alive.

Our blessing may be knowledge and we can help teach and advise those who do not know. Maybe it's a talent or a gift that we can use to lead others to the love, and mercy and grace of God. Whatever the blessing, God wants to us to pass it on so other lives can be transformed and brought to a knowledge of God's abundant life through Christ Jesus.

The blessing of Christ is God's ultimate blessing; "For God so loved the world, that He gave His only Son, that whosoever believes in Him shall not perish but have everlasting life"! It's not just a concept or a theory, it is truth. The Apostle Paul, filled with the joy of this greatest blessing of life through Christ, declared "Thanks be to God for his indescribable gift!"

Christ came to bring healing and forgiveness to a world that had not heard from God in nearly 400 years. It is spoken of in Romans 4:7 – "Blessed are those whose lawless deeds have been forgiven, and whose sins have been covered. Blessed is the man whose sin the Lord will not take into account".

God chose to pour out His greatest blessing through Christ as Paul says in Ephesians 1:3 "Praise be to the God and Father of our Lord Jesus Christ, who has blessed us in the heavenly realms with every spiritual blessing in Christ." Jesus was the channel of God's blessing to the world. Every blessing we have should draw us closer to God through Christ. We don't use Christ to get God's blessings, we use God's blessing to exalt and bring others to Him.

Let me give you just another way in which we are blessed; Jesus said to his disciples, "Blessed are your eyes because they see, and blessed are your ears because they hear." I am blessed and many of you are blessed because we have been given spiritual understanding and the wisdom of God's Word. In the Parable of the Sower for example, he said "the man who hears the word and understands it produces a crop yielding a hundred, sixty, or thirty times what was sown." In the Parable of the Talents we are admonished to use what we are given wisely in order to bring an increase of blessing. In the story of the sheep and the goats, Jesus said "Come, you who are blessed by my Father"…Why were they blessed?...Because as Jesus said: "I was hungry and you gave me something to eat, I was thirsty and you gave me drink, I was a stranger and you invited me in, I was sick and you looked after me." Why are they blessed? Because they were using whatever blessing – gift - or talent they had been given to bless others! "He who refreshes others will himself be refreshed!"

As Christ prepared to return to the Father in Luke 24:50, it says "When he had led them to the vicinity of Bethany, he lifted up his hands and blessed them!" The blessing of the Lord is never to be taken lightly, nor is it to be wasted on ourselves. If the disciples had not allowed the blessings of Christ to flow through them, we would not be here today. We are the product of God's blessing through someone who allowed themselves to be channels of those blessings to build a church in order to worship God; to reach others for His glory! If we truly feel blessed, can we do anything less? May all who have gone before us find us faithful! If He reigns, it pours!

1 Peter 1:13 – 2:3 – "Therefore, with minds that are alert and fully sober, set your hope on the grace to be brought to you when Jesus Christ is revealed at his coming. As obedient children, do not conform to the evil desires you had when you lived in ignorance. But just as he who called you is holy, so be holy in all you do; for it is written: "Be holy, because I am holy." Since you call on a Father who judges each person's work impartially, live out your time as foreigners here in reverent fear. For you know that it was not with perishable things such as silver or gold that you were redeemed from the empty way of life handed down to you from your ancestors, but with the precious blood of Christ, a lamb without blemish or defect. He was chosen before the creation of the world, but was revealed in these last times for your sake. Through him you believe in God, who raised him from the dead and glorified him, and so your faith and hope are in God. Now that you have purified yourselves by obeying the truth so that you have sincere love for each other, love one another deeply, from the heart. For you have been born again, not of perishable seed, but of imperishable, through the living and enduring word of God. For, "All people are like grass, and all their glory is like the flowers of the field; the grass withers and the flowers fall, but the word of the Lord endures forever." And this is the word that was preached to you. Therefore, rid yourselves of all malice and all deceit, hypocrisy, envy, and slander of every kind. Like newborn babies, crave pure spiritual milk, so that by it you may grow up in your salvation, now that you have tasted that the Lord is good."

When it comes to the Christians life and lifestyle, there is a good admonishment in 2 Corinthians 13:5 that we should look at often which says, "Examine yourselves to see whether you are in the faith; test yourselves. Do you not realize that Christ Jesus is IN you...unless of course, you fail the test?" Now, what is the "test"? I believe the test involves two things; *change* and *fruit*. Scripture itself testifies to the fact that if there is no change, there is no Christ – if there is no fruit, there is no Spirit!

I have been looking at various scriptures, all of which talk about "change or fruit" in the life of a Christian. I have learned that these are things that:

#1 God demands or commands;
#2 God desires and will do if we allow Him;
#3 Happen because we are born again;
#4 Only happen because of our will (we must make the effort and be consistent.)

Romans 12:2 says "Do not conform any longer to the pattern of this world, but be transformed by the renewing of your mind." There are three reasons it begins in the mind; One, so we will be able to "test and approve what God's will is" Two, because you can't put new wine into old wineskins...it will "blow their minds" and, three because when we change our thinking, it changes the way we feel, (affects our emotions) which in turn affects our will or our actions. The only way of real change is God's way – from the inside out!

God is in the business of "Extreme makeovers" - If there ever were scriptures that speak of change these are the ones:

2 Corinthians 5:17; "Therefore, if any man be in Christ, he is a new creature; old things are passed away; behold, all things become new!"

Matthew 7:16-20; "By their fruit you will recognize them. Do people pick grapes from thornbushes, or figs from thistles? Likewise, every good tree bears good fruit, but a bad tree bears bad fruit. A good tree cannot bear bad fruit, and a bad tree cannot bear good fruit. Every tree that does not bear good fruit is cut down and thrown into the fire. Thus, by their fruit you will recognize them."

John 13:34-35; "A new command I give you: Love one another. As I have loved you, so you must love one another. By this everyone will know that you are my disciples, if you love one another."

John 14:23-24 – "Jesus replied, "Anyone who loves me will obey my teaching. My Father will love them, and we will come to them and make our home with them. Anyone who does not love me will not obey my teaching. These words you hear are not my own; they belong to the Father who sent me."

John 15:5-8 – "I am the vine; you are the branches. If you remain in me and I in you, you will bear much fruit; apart from me you can do nothing. If you do not remain in me, you are like a branch that is thrown away and withers; such branches are picked up, thrown into the fire and burned. If you remain in me and my words remain in you, ask whatever you wish, and it will be done for you. This is to my Father's glory, that you bear much fruit, showing yourselves to be my disciples."

"Love" is the result of "change" in all three areas of our inner being; the mind, the heart, which in turn change our actions; and it is the first "fruit" of the Spirit. It is the fruit of the Spirit that will manifest itself when Christ is IN us. No change? No Christ! No fruit? No Spirit.

There are those who think if they *BELIEVE* the right thing that makes them okay with God. However, if what we believe (which is what we think or what is in our heads) never reaches our hearts, it is useless. The Pharisees believed a lot of right things, but Jesus had a problem with them!

There are also some who think that if they *DO* the right things, they are o.k. with God. "I attend church; give tithes and offerings; read my Bible now and then..." Just doing right things won't do it either - "any who say to me Lord, Lord", didn't we do this or didn't we do that…and Jesus said to them "Depart from me, I never knew you." (Matthew 7:23)

There are also those who think because they *DON'T do* certain things, they are right with God. "Well, I don't cuss, drink, smoke, or chew and I don't go with girls that do!" There were a lot of things the Pharisees didn't do, they were very righteous, but Jesus called them "white washed tombs." What God says in His Word is "They honor me with their lips, but their HEARTS are far from me."

Does God care about what we believe? (Yes) Does he care about the things we DO? (Yes) Does he care about the things we DON"T do? Of course! But, all of those things must stem from a heart that loves God because it's that love that will influence every aspect of our lives. "Man sees the outside, but God sees the heart!" (see Mathew 23:28)

Finally, I learned that all of this "change" either comes because God does it automatically, or because of the Holy Spirit convicting us and enabling us to change and produce fruit. It is all part of the process we call "sanctification". "It is God who works IN you to WILL and to ACT according to His good purpose". (Philippians 2:13)

We must hunger and long for the Word of God that will teach us the difference between truth and error, which will teach us the very mind and heart of God. As we walk by the power of the Holy Spirit, as we make the choice to put off the old and put on the new, we will become spiritually mature, sound, wholesome and healthy. We must long for the Word of God. And he will put that longing in our hearts.

Don't try to do it mechanically because it will taste sour if you do. We must long for it!

Peter's desire for his spiritual children is that they may grow in respect to their salvation if they have tasted of the kindness of the Lord. That's the process of sanctification. There is a difference between "change" and "growth" they are not the same. Growth is like a ship on a voyage; slow, steady progress toward the destination of maturity; change is more radical and critical. It's like the captain of the ship shouting; "Quick, start bailing, we're taking on water, and if we don't do something we're gonna go down!"

Growth is about improving who we are; change is about becoming someone different. Growth usually concerns addition – "Make every effort to add to your faith…goodness, knowledge, self-control, perseverance, godliness, brotherly kindness, and love." (2 Peter 1:5) Change is more about elimination of things that are damaging; "put off" - "put to death" – "crucify" – "rid yourselves of" – such things as; and then the list goes on…most of which are an act of our will. Yes, God will help us to change, but He never forces himself upon us…He will only do what we allow and ask Him to do. He does it by the power within us, but we must work "with" Him. "*With* God nothing is impossible!"

Romans 7:15-18 – "I do not understand what I do. For what I want to do I do not do, but what I hate I do. And if I do what I do not want to do, I agree that the law is good. As it is, it is no longer I myself who do it, but it is sin living in me. For I know that good itself does not dwell in me, that is, in my sinful nature. For I have the desire to do what is good, but I cannot carry it out."

In Robert Louis Stevenson's classic story of Dr. Jekyll and Mr. Hyde, a mild mannered Dr. would drink a potion and change from a sweet innocent bookkeeper type into a hideous monster. When the potion wore off, He would feel very ashamed and say "I just can't believe that was inside of me!" "I can't believe I would do those things!" However, even though he knew it was wrong, he was strangely drawn to drink the potion again and again. There was this on and off craving...and an on and off feeling of power and guilt..."I want to do right, but I can't seem to control this desire".

Have you ever felt like Jekyll and Hyde? We do something and then think "O why did I do that?" Or "Why did I say that!" We know we were wrong, but we discover that there is a big gap between knowing and doing; between our thoughts and our actions. Paul struggled with this same issue.

I Think that most people would agree that Paul probably was about as successful a Christian as you could find in the art of living the New Life in Christ Jesus, otherwise he could not say with confidence "Follow me" – or follow my example – "as I follow Christ." But it took something - some kind of change - to get Paul from where he is in this scripture, to being an example to follow in the Christian life. What was it? Change! As it concerns change in our lives, someone once said; "I'm not what I ought to be, and, I'm not what I want to be but thank God - I'm not what I use to be!"

You can't try to suppress your will and make yourself change! Just ask any smoker, alcoholic, or anyone who has ever made a New Year's resolution! Usually after repeated failure, we decide, "Well, if I can't change, then I'll just stop trying!" "I just don't have enough "willpower!" Jesus said in Matthew 26:41 "The spirit is willing, but the flesh is weak." The problem is that we "quit trying" in the flesh! (Our will power)

This scripture will cause problems toward understanding, if it is perceived ONLY through the doctrine of the believer's walk of victory in the power of Christ. Those truths tell of the believer's power through the Holy Spirit, the defeat of the enemies power, and how we can do all things through Christ who strengthens us. And of course that is all absolutely true - if we are walking in the Spirit – if we are being spirit led. But, we need to look at what Paul is saying about the sinful nature and how it co-exists in our lives even as "new creations in Christ."

What that means is even though we are Christians, we still spend a lot of time "walking in the flesh" rather than the Spirit. So, this struggle causes tension and we live as though we are having a "tug of war" with our spiritual nature. No matter how much we try to please God and to be conformed to the image of Christ, we keep coming up short.

If we were to stop at this point we are left with a pretty dismal and depressing picture of a war of hopeless conflict and tension between the flesh and the spirit. Thankfully, we are not left to dangle in despair, because all that Paul has announced has set the stage for his question as, he says, "Who will rescue me from this body of death?"…And then, he gives us the answer – "Thanks be to God-- through Jesus Christ our Lord..."

Deliverance from our sinful nature does not come through law, personal power, self resolve, or separation or a change of environment. All that has been said up to this point has been said to say this: Although both natures co-exist together in tension and conflict, only the stronger one will reign and rule in dominance. The stronger one will be the one that we attend to and spend the most time with. The stronger one will be the one that is fed, nourished and nurtured…the stronger one is the one that wins over our "wanna"!

God has given us great disciplines in which our new created spiritual nature may grow in the grace and the knowledge of God. Staying in His Word, prayer, fellowship, worship, service with a heart consistently filled with praise and thankfulness--- will see the presence, power and peace of our Lord enlarged and magnified within the believer's mind and heart. The more time we spend seeking the Holy Spirit's leading and direction, the more the Holy Spirit will occupy the desires, the reasoning, and the choices one makes, as the will seeks to please God.

The first announcement that Paul makes is that he is unspiritual, carnal and a slave to sin as perceived from within his sinful nature. When Paul says that he "is sold as a slave to sin" he simply means, that as a creature of the "sinful nature", he is subject to sin, a slave to sin in his sinful nature, capable of sinning, guilty of sinning, influenced by sin and cannot free himself - by himself - of sin and of falling short of God's glory. It goes to the scripture that says "no man can have two masters"...It's only when we decide to have one master, that we begin the journey to true change and the expression of fruit in our lives; love, joy, peace, patience, kindness, gentleness, self-control.

Perhaps it comes down to the words of Joshua...."Choose this day whom you will serve, as for me and my house---we shall serve the Lord."

I guess the word for this lesson on change would be "focus". What is the real focus of your life? If you were to keep a spiritual journal, how much time do you spend seeking and feeding and following your spiritual nature? An hour on Sunday? – Ten minutes a day? Real change means always having the right focus.

Ephesians 1:15-17 – "For this reason, ever since I heard about your faith in the Lord Jesus and your love for all God's people, I have not stopped giving thanks for you, remembering you in my prayers. I keep asking that the God of our Lord Jesus Christ, the glorious Father, may give you the Spirit of wisdom and revelation, so that you may know him better."

God's Word has a lot to say about knowledge, and the different forms and subjects of knowledge, and today we are going to look at what the Bible calls the "knowledge of God". Not knowing what God knows, but knowledge about God...or knowing God. Our scripture has to do with knowing some things about God, but we have to start from the beginning because of the first words of verse 15 – "For this reason" - So, we have to know first of all what Paul is talking about. For what reason?

How many spiritual blessings can we find here in these verses?

* He "chose us to be holy and blameless in His sight". (by the way, "to be" means this is a result of – not the basis for...)
* He "predestined us to be adopted as his sons – through Christ" (means nothing more than what it says!)
* "we have redemption" – "the forgiveness of sins" (by grace)
* "made known to us the 'mystery of Christ' (that is a blessing many don't enjoy.)
* "marked in him with a seal, the promised Holy Spirit" (you could call it a security deposit.)
"For this reason" – (because of all that or for all these reasons) "that the God of our Lord Jesus Christ, the glorious Father, may give to you the S*pirit of wisdom and of revelation, so that you may know Him better..."*

In other words, Paul is praying for the Ephesians the most important prayer any Believer can pray for another Believer; that God would take them deeper and deeper into an intimate knowledge of Himself. Man's chief end is to know God and to enjoy Him forever. It was determined in the Westminster Catechism; but Paul knew and taught that basic truth long before that was ever written.

He says, "that the God of our Lord Jesus Christ, the Father of glory, may give to you the Spirit of wisdom and of revelation in the **knowledge** of Him." Now something that surprised me about the various translations is that only the NIV translates verse 17 to say "the Spirit of wisdom and revelation" giving the word 'Spirit' a capital "S". The same Greek word is used for spirit throughout the New Testament, whether referring to the Holy Spirit or the spirit of man. The application of it is generally determined by the context. For example, chapter 1:13 uses the term Holy Spirit and that makes it quite obvious. But over in chapter 2, verse 18, when Paul says that we all have our access in one Spirit to the Father, it is understood that he again is referring to the Holy Spirit. So looking closely at verse 17, I have to say that the wording of it and in the context of what Paul is praying for the Ephesians, is for something that only the Holy Spirit of God can give. He is praying and asking God for this particular thing because he is praying for "spiritual wisdom and revelation" that can only come from God's Holy Spirit.

Now does that mean he's praying for God to give them the Holy Spirit? No, because he's writing to believers. They have the Holy Spirit since their salvation. What he is praying for simply, is the

Holy Spirit's help and continued unction in bringing to these faithful believers an ever greater wisdom and revelation in their knowledge of God.

When was the last time you prayed for the spiritual growth and well-being of another Christian? I wonder how many of us would even think to pray for one another that the Holy Spirit would give them wisdom and revelation in the knowledge of God? Some things we can pray for each other and never have to wonder if we are praying for a legitimate need or not. For instance, I can pray verse 18 - that "the Lord will enlighten the eyes of your heart, so that you may know what is the hope of His calling, and what are the riches of the glory of His inheritance in the saints, and what is the surpassing greatness of His power toward us who believe;" I can pray that the Lord will give you an ever greater hunger for His word, and that He will use your study to draw you ever closer to Himself, and that as you grow in the grace and knowledge of Him you will be used of Him to illuminate the world around you." How many of us pray that kind of prayer for one another?

When we pray this way, we're asking God to give us and give our fellow believers something that is only available to us who have the Holy Spirit of God. The point is this; Man in his natural mind cannot begin to comprehend God. In fact, one basic truth that the scriptures teach us from beginning to end, is that apart from the Spirit and spiritual birth, God is infinitely and eternally out of man's grasp. "Man does not accept the things of the Spirit of God; for they are foolishness to him, and he cannot understand them, because they are spiritually discerned." (1st. Corinthians 2:14) Paul is, in effect, repeating Jesus' teaching when He told the Pharisee Nicodemus, "...unless one is born again he cannot **see** the kingdom of God." Man cannot have the knowledge of God apart from God's Spirit; the wisdom, the teaching, and the understanding of the things of the Spirit.

Here is probably the clearest and best example. The disciples walked and talked with Jesus for over three years. They were with Him constantly, listening to Him teach, seeing His miracles, asking Him questions, seeing Him in all the aspects and circumstances of life. But they did not understand. They did not perceive His purpose in coming, until after the resurrection...and even then they continued to ask questions that exposed their ignorance. "We were hoping that it was He who was going to redeem Israel"...They asked him; "Lord, is it at this time you are restoring the kingdom to Israel?" It wasn't until they were gathered in the upper room, and they were all filled with the Holy Spirit that they stepped out onto the streets of Jerusalem with a greater knowledge and power.

Now I want you to take notice here... they weren't given a crash course in theology. They didn't stay sequestered in the upper room for another thirteen weeks while Jesus appeared to them with a dry erase board and a box of scrolls and taught them doctrine and homiletics and how to properly apply the scriptures...They had a certain knowledge, a learning that He had stored up in them while He was with them, but they had no revelation of the Spirit, until He came and filled them; and baptized them, there in that upper room.

And when He did, these disciples who only days before stood gazing into the sky as He ascended...now stepped immediately out of the upper room and preached a Holy Spirit inspired sermon that had even those who crucified their Lord crying, "What must we do to be saved?"

So you see, it is not enough to have just a head-knowledge of Jesus. To examine Him and scrutinize His word and His actions and think to understand Him that way. Our relationship to Him must be based on the revelation of Himself through His Spirit to our spirits; it will only be in the spirit and by the Spirit of wisdom and revelation; as Paul prays; that we will begin to understand His mission in the world, His purpose in us; and that we begin to know the Father.

I want to finish today by giving you an excerpt from D. Martin Lloyd-Jones' commentary on this verse. I enjoyed what he said and I want to share it with you;

"We have been considering one of the most important doctrines of the Christian faith. The Protestant Reformers used to tell their hearers that there is a double action of the Holy Spirit. There is the 'Testimonium Spiritus Externus' - the Spirit that is in the Word, as it were, the Spirit that inspired the men who produced the Word. That is essential. But it is not enough. Before I know that this is God's Word and God's truth, before I can read the Bible and discover health and food for my soul, something additional is necessary - the 'Testimonium Spiritus Internus'. The Spirit in the reader! And without the Spirit in him no man will be able to understand the meaning of the Word. The two operations are absolutely essential."

In other words we have seen that the Apostle Paul prays for the Ephesian believers that the God of our Lord Jesus Christ, the Father of glory, may give them 'the Spirit of wisdom (the Spirit in the Word) and 'the Spirit of revelation' (the Spirit in the believer) taking the Word and from it revealing a knowledge of God in all His glory.

A Lack of Knowledge

Hosea 4:1-7 – "Hear the word of the LORD, you Israelites, because the LORD has a charge to bring against you who live in the land: "There is no faithfulness, no love, no acknowledgment of God in the land. There is only cursing, lying and murder, stealing and adultery; they break all bounds, and bloodshed follows bloodshed. Because of this the land dries up, and all who live in it waste away; the beasts of the field, the birds in the sky and the fish in the sea are swept away. "But let no one bring a charge, let no one accuse another, for your people are like those who bring charges against a priest. You stumble day and night, and the prophets stumble with you. So I will destroy your mother— my people are destroyed from lack of knowledge. "Because you have rejected knowledge, I also reject you as my priests; because you have ignored the law of your God, I also will ignore your children. The more priests there were, the more they sinned against me; they exchanged their glorious God for something disgraceful."

In the Old Testament, the nation of Israel was called to be a nation of priests. Israel was to be a bridge between the nations and God. This is what the church today is supposed to do; bridge the gap between the world (those who do not know God) and God. We are to be "his ambassadors" the Word says, "reconciling the world to God." (2 Corinthians 18-20) Now, 1 Peter 2:9 says "But you are a chosen race, a royal priesthood, a holy nation, a people for God's own possession, that you may proclaim the excellencies of Him who has called you out of darkness into His marvelous light."

The nation of Israel was accepting the ways of the world. They were not carrying out God's will because they were pushing God aside and were being absorbed by the world. The people were worshipping other things besides God. The people were living in religious hypocrisy. The nation was going through the motions of religion…Does this sound familiar?

The problem is a lack of knowledge. The problem is that we do not know God. Where some parts of Scripture emphasize the "fear of God," Hosea emphasizes a knowledge of God. When we lack knowledge about God, we do not – and in fact, cannot - develop a relationship with Him. Our relationships are built upon the foundation of knowledge. A lot of marriages fail because the relationship is just based on emotions or the satisfaction of needs. To really love someone you really have to know them.

The Israelites did not have an intimate knowledge of God or a relationship with God, and, Hosea lists six things that resulted:

1. NO FAITHFULNESS

The people were struggling with their faithfulness to God because of the lack of knowledge and because of the lack of a relationship with God. As God's chosen people looked around them, they saw the pagans worshipping. Pagan worship looked fun to them; it was loose and just about anything was allowed. There were really no rules. This looked good to the people of God; they constantly struggled with Baal worship and other forms of idolatry. What would you compare that to today?

We will struggle with being faithful to God because we will have no foundation for our faithfulness. If you do not know God, what is it that keeps you in line? Hebrews 11:6 "And without faith it is impossible to please Him, for he who comes to God must believe that He is and that He is a rewarder of those who seek Him." How can we know, much less please or even desire to please someone with whom we have no relationship?

2. NO KINDNESS

Luke 6:27 "But I say to you who hear, love your enemies, do good to those who hate you." How many of us want to do this? How many of us want to be kind to people who do not like us? Jesus told us that if we are only good to those who are good to us, then we are no better than the pagans who do the same. Do you find it hard to be kind to some people? As you grow closer to Jesus, you will find that being kind to people becomes so much easier. If we are not kind, we will not attract people to Jesus. I remember the story that Jesus told of the Good Samaritan. Remember, a man was injured, the priest and the Levite walked right by the man, but the Samaritan stopped and helped the man. The punch line was that the Jews hated the Samaritan's so this story really struck a nerve with them. When people in your community need kindness and compassion, I hope that it is God's people who are there. Showing kindness to people will go a long way. One of the benefits of knowing God is that we will start seeing people the way that Jesus saw them, because we as we grow in our knowledge and love for Jesus, we are being transformed into His image. (2 Corinthians 3:18)

3. IGNORANCE

This passage says that the people did not have knowledge of God, this is ignorance. Ignorance breeds even more ignorance. Ignorance is dangerous. If we are ignorant of something, we will believe anything about it. The Constitution of the United States is a good example. How many of you know that the Constitution speaks about the separation of church and state? It does have that phrase in it doesn't it? No, it does not. We have a whole nation of people who think that is in there, so based on that assumption, we are allowing a minority the power to remove God in our society. When we are ignorant of God's word, we will not know when we are being sold a bill of goods. What if the church buys into the thought that all roads lead to heaven, so there is really no difference in religions and that doctrinal differences mean nothing? When the people are ignorant, they will believe everything except the truth!

4. A LIFE OF SIN... VS 2-3

A lack of knowledge makes us ignorant to the truth. We do not know what God wants us to do in our lives. If we do not know God's word, then how are we supposed to live for Him? Ignorance of God and His word leads to a life of sin. Notice the items mentioned here... They are all direct violations of God's Law. The "People of God" were being swept away by the sinful life-styles of the pagans around them. Is this happening today? Why is this happening to the church? We have allowed the teachings of the world to infiltrate the church. 1John 2:15 "Do not love the world nor the things in the world. If anyone loves the world, the love of the Father is not in him". I'm afraid we have fallen too much in love with the world and its ways to keep it out of us.

5. NO REPROOF

Romans 1:32 and "although they know the ordinance of God, that those who practice such things are worthy of death, they not only do the same, but also give hearty approval to those who practice them." We have a whole nation that wonders why things are getting so bad socially, and when we tell them why, we are told we are intolerant, narrow-minded, bigots. There are absolutes even if over 70% of the people say there are none. If God says it is wrong, it is wrong for everyone.

6. FUTURE GENERATIONS ARE AFFECTED

Ignorance breeds ignorance. God says to the Israelites that He was going to turn from the children of the people because the more they had, the more they sinned. We are raising a society of people who know little to nothing about God and we will pay, and are paying the price for that. The nation of Israel suffered because one generation did not teach the other. If we – who sit in the church - do not know God, how in the world will we teach our children, and how will they teach their children?

God's word to us is the same today as it was then;

"My people perish from a lack of knowledge."

Ephesians 1:1-14 – "Praise be to the God and Father of our Lord Jesus Christ, who has blessed us in the heavenly realms with every spiritual blessing in Christ. For he chose us in him before the creation of the world to be holy and blameless in his sight. In love he predestined us for adoption to sonship through Jesus Christ, in accordance with his pleasure and will— to the praise of his glorious grace, which he has freely given us in the One he loves. In him we have redemption through his blood, the forgiveness of sins, in accordance with the riches of God's grace that he lavished on us. With all wisdom and understanding, he made known to us the mystery of his will according to his good pleasure, which he purposed in Christ, to be put into effect when the times reach their fulfillment—to bring unity to all things in heaven and on earth under Christ. In him we were also chosen, having been predestined according to the plan of him who works out everything in conformity with the purpose of his will, in order that we, who were the first to put our hope in Christ, might be for the praise of his glory. And you also were included in Christ when you heard the message of truth, the gospel of your salvation. When you believed, you were marked in him with a seal, the promised Holy Spirit, who is a deposit guaranteeing our inheritance until the redemption of those who are God's possession—to the praise of his glory."

There is an unusual structure in this passage of scripture. From Verse 3 through Verse 14 in the Greek text (not in the English) it is written in one complete, unbroken sentence filled with many descriptive phrases brought in to amplify and enrich it. It's almost as though Paul is taking a walk through a treasure chamber, like those of the Pharaohs of Egypt, describing what he sees. He starts out with the most immediate and evident fact and tells us what that is. Then something else comes into view and he puts that in. And glory flashes upon glory here until he has this tremendously complicated sentence which includes vast and almost indescribable riches.

This is the way God builds truth. One truth leads into the next and all truth is interrelated somehow, and all truth is based or centered around God. There is a rather simplifying division of this passage, however, and that is, that these blessings gather about the Persons of the Trinity. There is the work of the Father, the work of the Son, and the work of the Holy Spirit:

In Verses 3-6 you have the work of the Father: Then, in Verses 7-12, you have that which relates to the Son: Finally, in Verses 13 and 14, you have the work of the Holy Spirit:

Remember that these are all available to us in the "heavenly realms" That is not heaven; it does not mean they are only available in heaven when you die. No, "in the heavenly realms" is a reference to the invisible realities of our life now. It reaches on into eternity, yes, but it is something to be experienced now, in the inner life. He is talking about our thought-life, our attitudes, our emotions, our inner life where we live, where we feel conflict and pressure, struggle and disaster. He calls them "*spiritual* blessings in Christ"...What does that mean?

It is in these areas of our inner life that we are exposed to the attack of the principalities and powers which are mentioned in Chapter 6, those dark spirits in high places who get to us, and depress us, and frighten us, and make us anxious or hostile or angry. It is the realm of conflict, but it is also the realm where God can release us and deliver us, and where the Spirit of God reaches us at the seat of our intellect, our emotions and our will. It is the realm of those deep, surging urges which rise within us and can create either a restlessness or a sense of peace, depending on the source from which they come. So don't read this as though it were something out in heaven somewhere, someday. These blessings that Paul gives us and which we will be looking more closely at, are ours in our inner experience, now, if we are in Jesus Christ...This is the "package" that it all comes in – "Christ".

If you are not a Christian you cannot possibly claim these benefits. They are not yours, they don't belong to you. You cannot buy them, you cannot discover them. There is no way you can claim them unless you are in Christ. But, if you are "in Christ" there is nothing to keep you from having all of them, every moment of every day. That is why it is so important that we discover what they are.

You see, these are much more than mere doctrinal or mere theological ideas. They are facts, they are foundational truths. And, unless we understand those facts, we can't utilize them, we can't benefit from them. I would even say that these great facts are so revolutionary, so radical, that we hesitate to believe them! And even more-so, we hesitate to apply them to ourselves despite the fact that they are true. The reason we hesitate is that we have such distorted ideas of what these words mean. We think of words like "holy and blameless" and we think that holiness is all about being absolutely sinless and pure...and we don't want to claim that for ourselves. But it is not that at all. Holiness means "wholeness," and *wholeness* means "to be restored to the originally intended function; to be put to the proper use, that's all. Physical wholeness prevails when the body works the way it was supposed to. When your whole being functions the way it was intended to function, you are holy.

It is when we begin to understand these words that we can apply them and accept them. Now let's look at the other one, *"blameless"*. Most people refuse to think of themselves as blameless because they know that they have done many things for which they ought to be blamed. That is, they have made choices, deliberate choices, against right, against God, and even against the knowledge of the consequences. But we confuse this word with another, because it is not *sinless*. Never having done anything wrong is sinless. But, the Bible says you can be sinful and still be blameless. Do you know how? By handling your sin in the right way. If you did something that injured someone else, and the full result of it was not visible to you when you did it, but afterward you saw how much you had hurt the person, and you acknowledged it, apologized to them, asked for forgiveness, and did what you could to restore it, then there would be nothing further you could do. From that point on you would be blameless. You would not be sinless -- you still did it -- but you also did all you could to handle it rightly, or to make it right.

The idea is the same with our offenses against God. What can you do about your sins? You can't go back and straighten it all out, no, but you can ask for and accept his forgiveness. You can acknowledge what you did and your need for forgiveness, you can seek to restore the relationship, and when you've done that, you're blameless! That is what God has chosen us to do -- to learn this wonderful process of being whole (holy) and blameless.

Notice that these things are to be *reckoned* true even though we don't feel that way. We need to accept the fact that God chose us "in Christ" to make us holy and blameless. And as we walk before him in his prescribed way, that is what we are; we ought to "reckon" that we are, and we ought to rejoice in that great fact.

Now look at the second great aspect which is recorded of the work of the Father, and which is related to the first, (Ephesians 1:5-6) Here is a partial explanation of how God takes care of all the past failures and the shame of our lives, in order to produce someone who is holy and blameless. It is by means of a "change" of family relationship. "He predestined us to be sons" ...Most of us are familiar with the process of adoption. Adoption means leaving one family and joining another. Leaving behind all that was involved in the first family and assuming the name, the characteristics, the resources, and the relationships of another family. We've been transferred and adopted into a new family. This is why we are called the "family of God."

Now, my question is: Are you enjoying your inheritance? Do you wake in the morning and remind yourself at the beginning of the day, "I'm a child of the Father...El Elyon...the "Most High God"..."I've been chosen by him to be a member of his family!" Because He chose me, He imparts to me His peace, His joy, and, His love, His resources, His knowledge and wisdom and much more. They are my inheritance from which I can draw every moment of life. And I have them no matter what my circumstances may be. In

His sight - through Jesus Christ His Son - I am holy and blameless!"
Well, I reckon it's true!

Ephesians - 1:15-18

The phrase, "For this reason," looks back upon the great previous passage from verse 3 through Verse 14, in which Paul has been outlining the great, fundamental facts about our faith.

He is writing to "the faithful in Christ Jesus" according to verse 1 of chapter one; and, he is convinced that they are Christians because of two things which have come to his attention -- their faith, and their love. That should be very insightful to us. A while back, we looked at how God measures a church, as well as how He measures our faith and growth as a Christian. It comes from this scripture - He has heard of the fact that they have confessed Christ and have great faith; But the thing that proves that their faith was true was the evidence of their love -- If our faith has not resulted in our becoming a more loving person, or at least growing in this direction, then it is not genuine faith. It is merely an intellectual acceptance, which means nothing. Both James and John stress this very fact in (James 2:14-17 & 1st.John 3:11-23) Read it.

Paul agrees. He has heard of their love, and so he is aware that their faith is genuine. In other words their faith has made a noticeable difference in their lives and their attitudes and their actions. And notice that it is love toward ALL the saints, not just toward some of them. Some saints are easy to love. Some are beautiful people, joyful and happy, and everybody likes to be around them. But Paul is struck by the fact that these Christians love all the saints, and, therefore, their love is not based upon people's personalities, their looks, nor upon their wealth; or anything else, rather, it is based upon the fact that they are Christians. They belong to the Lord Jesus; they are part of the family of God. This is something every Christian must learn. This is a truth of scripture; the knowledge of doctrine is never enough to enable one to grow up as a Christian. You can learn all that there is in the Bible, and be able to write a very profound and scholarly theological thesis on it, but if it hasn't reached the heart it is absolutely worthless.

A Truth known never changes anybody; it is truth done, truth which has flowed through the emotions and gripped the heart and thus motivated the will that makes a difference. Thus this passage beautifully takes into consideration the way God has made us. He has made us so that truth hits the mind first of all. We are exposed to the facts, to the truth, but that is never enough. There are some people who think that if you merely study your Bible and take the right courses and learn all these great facts, learn the doctrine, and the truth of the Scriptures, that is all you need. But just that much will never change anybody. But truth must somehow move from the head down to the heart. It must grip "the eyes of the heart," to use the beautiful figure that Paul employs, "I pray that the eyes of your heart may be enlightened"...Truth alone can be dull and academic and deadly. Your heart also must be stirred in order to motivate the will! Like the two disciples whom Jesus met on the road to Emmaus who said, "Did not our hearts burn within us while he talked to us on the road, while he opened to us the scriptures?" (Luke 24:32)

Paul then prays "that he may give you a spirit of wisdom and of revelation so that you may know Him better." Why does he say that? Because it's all about relationship, not just knowledge. Notice that he doesn't take it for granted that this is going to happen. This is not an automatic feature of the Christian life...He prays for it!

He goes on to pray; "having the eyes of your hearts enlightened, that you may know Him better, and the HOPE..." Then he tells us what the "hope" is; - "the riches of his glorious inheritance" and "his incomparably great power for us who believe." They have lost their sense of hope. They know it as a doctrine, but they have lost the experience of it, the emotions of it, the expectancy of it.

So Paul prays that God will enlighten their hearts so that they may know the hope of God's calling. Hope always concerns the future. These people obviously had lost their sense that anything happening now will affect the future. This happens to many of us. We all say we are waiting for the coming of the Lord, but it doesn't really turn us on very much. We know it as doctrine, but it isn't very exciting – right here, right now. How would it affect us if we knew Jesus was coming tomorrow? Yet scripture tells us that He could come any moment..."in the twinkling of an eye!"

There is one final element in Paul's request here -- that you may know "what is the immeasurable greatness of his power in us who believe" (Ephesians 1:19) Paul prays that Christians will get their eyes open, in a practical way, to the power available in them -- "that you may know what is the immeasurable greatness of his power *in us* (not up in heaven somewhere) – but *in us* who believe." The only

174

place this kind of power is ever going to be manifested is in you and me; in the church! So, this is what God is telling us. He has come to give us hope, and riches, and power -- power to be what he wants us to be, and power to do what He, wants us to do.

Psalms 139:13-16 – "For you created my inmost being;
you knit me together in my mother's womb.
I praise you because I am fearfully and wonderfully made;
your works are wonderful,
I know that full well.
My frame was not hidden from you
when I was made in the secret place,
when I was woven together in the depths of the earth.
Your eyes saw my unformed body;
all the days ordained for me were written in your book
before one of them came to be.

2 Peter 1:3-9 – "His divine power has given us everything we need for a godly life through our knowledge of him who called us by his own glory and goodness. Through these he has given us his very great and precious promises, so that through them you may participate in the divine nature, having escaped the corruption in the world caused by evil desires.

For this very reason, make every effort to add to your faith goodness; and to goodness, knowledge; and to knowledge, self-control; and to self-control, perseverance; and to perseverance, godliness; and to godliness, mutual affection; and to mutual affection, love. For if you possess these qualities in increasing measure, they will keep you from being ineffective and unproductive in your knowledge of our Lord Jesus Christ. But whoever does not have them is nearsighted and blind, forgetting that they have been cleansed from their past sins."

To begin my study for this series, I went to the dictionary to find the technical definition of the word intent. This is what I found:
INTENT = a determination to act in a certain way; Resolve...
RESOVLE = fixation of purpose; Resoluteness....
RESOLUTENESS = firm determination marked by boldness and steadfastness.

With these definitions, living an intentional life could be stated this way: An intentional life is one with purpose. The purpose is followed with a bold and steady determination until the desired outcome is realized. To make it easier to remember, I settled on this phrase: *"An intentional life has purpose, discipline and results."* The emphasis being on results!

Before we can jump into what I will simply define as the "eight areas of priorities" in life, we must first ask "Why is this an important issue"? The answer to that is simple: "If you always do what you have always done; You will always get what you have always got!" It is really about each one of us taking control of our lives and deter-mining our own happiness and well being, rather than allowing our lives to be controlled by other people, circumstances or forces.

The whole premise of the Intentional Life Plan is this; If we do not have an agenda for our lives, one will be provided for us—either by the events and circumstances of life itself, or by other people.

You see, to live intentionally means to live on purpose. It means that we are taking control and *determining how we will live our lives and spend our time, energy and resources.* Without such a plan, you could say that just the opposite of our phrase is true; "An UN-intentional life neither seeks nor has purpose, is very undisciplined, and will yield little if any – and usually the wrong results!" If that describes how you have been living, read on!

I want a lay a foundation for intentional living by considering three facts;

(a.) *God has a purpose and plan for every life*. And, that God's plan includes all areas of life. What I mean is this; we live compartment - alized lives. Each part being separate from the others, and yet at the same time being interconnected in the way each affects the other as they all affect our whole being; like interconnecting circles.

I have taken the liberty of breaking them down to eight categories...We have our:

(a.) Home or Family life
(b.) Spiritual life
(c.) Work life or Career
(d.) Our Recreational life,
(e.) Church life;
(f.) Intellectual life;
(g.) Financial life; and finally,
(h.) Our Physical/Health and well being.

But, one thing we need to know is that with God, there is no distinction between the differing areas of our lives. He's concerned with all of it. *He is concerned with the physical, mental and emotional well being in every area.* And, as we get further into the plan, you will see how one area affects the other, which in turn affects another, and so on. It is the way we were "knit together in the womb" you might say.

Not only does God have a plan for our lives but (b.) *God has a will for our lives*. Although they are closely related, I believe there is a slight difference. For instance, it was God's will for me to become a minister of His Word; and, how and where His will is carried out in my life is His plan.

God has a plan for every life, every person, has a part in God's will. However, because God has given us free will, His will is not always accomplished in our individual lives. That's because *Our wills determine whether or not God's purpose is accomplished in our lives.* Believe it or not, there are people who never accept Jesus as their savior; which is God's will. There are Christians who remain spiritually immature, and never reach the potential of God's plan for their lives.

(c.) GOD not only has a plan and a will, but *God has an intended outcome*—that man would enter into a loving relationship with HIM. This plan started in the Garden of Eden but was frustrated when Adam and Eve disobeyed God's command not to eat from one tree. Sin entered the world of mankind and ever since that time, God has worked to bring man back to himself; first with the Jewish people, then with the Gentiles. But it was Jesus who came to bring us back to God once and for all. "For God so loved the world that He gave His only Son; that whosoever believes in Him shall not perish but have everlasting life". If this verse were the only Bible we had, it would be all we need!

2 Cor. 5:17 tells us; "Therefore, if anyone is in Christ, he is a new creation; the old has gone, the new has come! All this is from God, who reconciled us to himself through Christ and gave us the ministry of reconciliation: that God was reconciling the world to himself in Christ, not counting men's sins against them. And he has committed to us the message of reconciliation. We are therefore Christ's ambassadors, as though God were making his appeal through us. We

implore you on Christ's behalf: Be reconciled to God. God made him who had no sin to be sin for us, so that in him we might become the righteousness of God." This is where it all starts, being "reconciled to God"! Even if you have been a Christian for many years, you may not have lived according to God's will and plan for your life. So, here is where it must begin for everyone, being "reconciled to God".

God desire's a loving - ever-growing - relationship with you and me. And, I don't say this because I am a minister, but because I know it to be true. This relationship with God is the most important thing you will ever do in life! It will not only save you and bring you peace and joy (the great stress busters!) it will greatly enhance all eight areas of your life I have mentioned. How much better is each area of our life if God is involved?

God has a plan, a will, and an intended outcome. Now the question is; what does all of this mean to you and me?

Remember, God does not divide our lives into different areas, he wants all of it. He wants our home life, our work life, our spiritual life, and even our recreational life to be directed by Him…and bring praise glory, and honor to Him. He has a plan and a purpose, He has a will and a desired outcome for every area of our lives, but it must be our desire, our will, and our *intention* to seek it, find it, and do it!

It doesn't matter how spiritual you act here in church. It doesn't matter how much money you give here. It doesn't matter how often you come here. It doesn't matter who your friends and family are. It doesn't matter if you're a member of the church. What matters is your answer to the question; "Do you really know God? Are you intentionally living the life he desires for you; the full, and abundant life? Or are you allowing circumstances, people, money, position, or anything besides God, dictate your life and your time for you?

I believe that living that way is the main cause of stress in our lives. We have all these things that we "intend" to do but don't or believe we can't...and they are a source of stress. We need a change! We need to take control!

John Maxwell has said; "Change is not a once and for all kind of thing - if only it were that easy. No, changing ourselves is a lifelong process. Not only that, but we must be intentional about how we want to change. I find that we often make two mistakes in this area. First, we often sit around and wait for God to change our circumstances. Second, we wait for circumstances to change our attitude and our behavior. Is it any wonder that some people change so little? Most people fail to see that life is moving on at a rapid speed. None of us have all the time we'd like to have...and, in fact, we are not getting any more...so we need to take control and make the best of the time we have. Someone once said that the only person who really wants change in the church are the wet babies!

If you see an area you need to change, CHANGE NOW. I'm not talking about cosmetic changes. That's where we change our talking but not our thinking, we change our environment instead of our expectations, our appearance instead of our attitudes, our business instead of our behavior, and our biases instead of our beliefs.

Rather than intentionally changing ourselves, too many of us are "wisher's" content with dreaming about the results we desire from life and wonder why they remain just that - "dreams, and wishes!"

If we desire God's best for our lives; if we desire to live with less stress; if we desire to change the results we are getting in the eight areas of life mentioned; then we must **intentionally** do it!

God operates in an intentional manner and I believe our lives will be better if we do also. Remember; If you always do what you have always done, you will always get what you have always got!

Mark 12:28-34 – "One of the teachers of the law came and heard them debating. Noticing that Jesus had given them a good answer, he asked him, "Of all the commandments, which is the most important?" "The most important one," answered Jesus, "is this: 'Hear, O Israel: The Lord our God, the Lord is one. Love the Lord your God with all your heart and with all your soul and with all your mind and with all your strength.' The second is this: 'Love your neighbor as yourself.' There is no commandment greater than these."

"Well said, teacher," the man replied. "You are right in saying that God is one and there is no other but him. To love him with all your heart, with all your understanding and with all your strength, and to love your neighbor as yourself is more important than all burnt offerings and sacrifices."

When Jesus saw that he had answered wisely, he said to him, "You are not far from the kingdom of God." And from then on no one dared ask him any more questions."

Today we will continue our series on Living an Intentional Life. I want to bring out once again the key words from the last lesson of introduction in describing an intentional life, and that is that an intentional life has purpose, discipline, and results. The reason to focus on living an intentional life is that if we don't have an agenda for our lives, one will be provided for us by our friends, our families, and other people, as well as by our circumstances...and that causes stress!! If we want to relieve stress and take control of our lives; then we need to find our purpose or our priorities in each of the eight areas of our lives; then produce a plan that will help us discipline ourselves to intentionally take control of those things which will produce results that will amaze us!

We need to define the areas of **stress** in our lives, which are usually our real priorities in each area that we would like to see happen, but never do, because we have allowed everything and everyone to set our agenda, day in and day out! We need to *seek and find those undone priorities* in each area of our lives such as our families, our work, our church, our physical health as well as our financial goals and dreams, and most of all we must make the decision to do something about taking control of this life that God has given us. We need to intentionally seek it, find it, and do it.

We need to first understand that we are talking about our present and our future, we can't change the past; but, we can change the future from this day forward. And, we can change every important area of our lives from this day forward, in ways that we never thought possible. We can get excited about life because we know we serve a God who is able to do "exceedingly, abundantly, more than we could ever ask, think, or dream!" His Word says that "with God, all things are possible!" The key word being "with". That's called a positive faith. It's a partnership! With that in mind, let's talk about the intentional spiritual life.

One of golf's immortal moments came when a Scotsman demonstrated the new game to President Ulysses Grant. Carefully placing the ball on the tee, he took a mighty swing...missed...his club hit the turf scattering dirt all over the President. With the ball still sitting on the tee, the man swung again, and again he missed. President Grant waited patiently through six tries and then quietly stated; "There seems to be a fair amount of exercise in the game…but I fail to see the purpose of the ball!"

For all the busyness and all the exercise in many of our lives, the question must be asked if we are getting anywhere? Is there any purpose? Are we hitting the ball or just beating the wind?

We need to intentionally focus on the priorities in life. Priorities are guides. They are tools that help us make sure attention is given to the things that need it; the important things that need attention first, and most! Life can be hectic and without priorities, important things can be easily neglected. The goal of this series is to help you - not just identify your priorities - but to actually develop a plan to accomplish them in each area mentioned. The number one priority in the spiritual area of our lives is a closer relationship with God. It is my conviction that to fall short in this area will leave us open to possible disaster in all the other areas of life.

Ironically, as with most priorities, it is easy to neglect the *discipline* needed to care for this relationship. It doesn't scream for attention. You can go through some days and hardly even think about God or your relationship with Him; except for an occasional Sunday. It is this danger that powerfully emphasizes its importance. Our relationship with God is one that requires constant maintenance, constant awareness, and must be a part of our daily living. We need to have some sort of daily time with God. Whether that time is in study, prayer, devotionals, meditating, or whatever, it is important that we take the time and make the time to do it.

Whether it is our spiritual area, our family area, our physical health area, or any of the eight, we all know people who are gonna do this and gonna do that, but this gets in the way; and that happened; the time wasn't right; and there is always a reason why they didn't accomplish what they "intended" to do. That's exactly what this is about! Purposely, or intentionally doing those things and not allowing "this" or "that" control our lives.

Jesus' words in Mark 12:31—"Love the Lord your God with all your heart, soul, mind and strength; and Love your neighbor as yourself" are the types of things that we could write on a piece of paper and then list an endless list of ways to do just that. But, as with all eight areas of life, unless we make an intentional plan; a spiritual "time budget"; we will not do much of anything toward loving God or our neighbor. It will just be another one of those things we "intended" to do. And, "If we always do what we have always done; we will always get what we have always got!"

First on our list must be <u>Prayer</u>. We can't have a relationship with someone we never talk to! Many marriage relationships are not what they should be or can be, because people don't talk to each other enough. Spending daily time in prayer must become a priority. How about, keeping a personal prayer journal containing all types of prayers; petitions; requests; thanksgiving; and intercession; and highlighting answered prayer as we see God working.

Along that same vein may be time in a daily devotional and meditating on the Word. Another thing on our list might be a way in which we can serve God in the church by using our talents and gifts. Or how about - loving our neighbor by intentionally sharing our faith and inviting them over for a meal or even inviting them to church?

(Now that's a novel idea!) You may ask, "What does this have to do with improving my spiritual area of life?" It must begin with "Love the Lord your God...and your neighbor as yourself!"

If we truly want to draw closer to God in our spiritual life, then we will intentionally discipline ourselves accordingly. The more time we spend with God and loving and serving one another, the better our spiritual relationships will be.

Remember, the UN-intentional life has no purpose, no discipline, and ultimately no results! We need to ask ourselves; "What is the result of what I have been doing up till now?" If it's not working, then we need to intentionally make a change.

Time is the biggest factor to be disciplined in our relationship with God. Time for prayer; time for the word; time for church. We all get 7 days...We all get 168 hours...a week. We have to choose how we spend that time. Our wills must be disciplined, or someone or something else will choose for us. When it comes to time, I can tell you this; if we make time, it will take time. In other words none of the changes we make in each area of our life is going to happen over-night. However, if we make the time, and discipline ourselves, it will soon become a habit and we will see results! Results that will change our lives from this day on!

Part of the Intentional Living Plan is intentionally setting a time budget in each area of our lives. Not finding time to do everything we want to do, but **making** time to do that which is most important. I mean - actually taking a calendar and marking down times, dates, hours, minutes, whatever it takes to make the time to do those things that we find are really important to us and we never seem to have enough time for. It may be a simple task like feeding our intellect by reading a book, or it may be a major thing like spending quality time with our spouse. It requires finding those important things in our lives and then focusing on intentionally **making** the time to do them - put them on the calendar!

I said that God is concerned with every area of our lives...but he is most concerned with this one; our relationship with Him. He desires for our will to be in line with His will and for us to intentionally live the life he has planned for us. A full, happy, abundant, stress-free life. He wants me to love him with all my heart, soul, mind and strength and He wants this to be displayed in practical ways in my everyday life. He wants me to love and treat others as I would hope to be treated. And, he wants this also to be displayed in practical ways in my everyday life. The best thing I can do to help my relationship with God...is to have one!

Make the time to get to know God on a daily basis. Read the Bible - Get a version you can really understand. (There are no anointed versions.) Pray—just talk to God--Tell God how you feel. Ask God to let his will be done in your life. Ask God to meet your needs. Ask Him to forgive your sin. Ask Him to help you fight temptation. Tell him when your angry, tell him when you are happy, tell him when you are disappointed or you don't understand. You can't tell God anything He doesn't already know! He just wants to spend time with you. Put a better relationship with God at the top of your priority list.

I have given you this definition of an intentional life: "An intentional life is one with purpose that is followed by a steady disciplined determination until the desired results are realized." Make that the definition of your relationship with God. Pursue his purposes with a bold and steady determination until you become exactly what he wants you to become. Remember that it's a process; it's a marathon, not a sprint. It will not happen overnight.

God promised that he will never give up on us. With that assurance, I would ask you today to renew your commitment to having an intentional relationship with God...Right now, why not tell Him you are going to spend more time with Him?

Ephesians 5:22-6:3 – "Wives, submit yourselves to your own husbands as you do to the Lord. For the husband is the head of the wife as Christ is the head of the church, his body, of which he is the Savior. Now as the church submits to Christ, so also wives should submit to their husbands in everything.

Husbands, love your wives, just as Christ loved the church and gave himself up for her to make her holy, cleansing her by the washing with water through the word, and to present her to himself as a radiant church, without stain or wrinkle or any other blemish, but holy and blameless. In this same way, husbands ought to love their wives as their own bodies. He who loves his wife loves himself. After all, no one ever hated their own body, but they feed and care for their body, just as Christ does the church— for we are members of his body. "For this reason a man will leave his father and mother and be united to his wife, and the two will become one flesh." This is a profound mystery—but I am talking about Christ and the church. However, each one of you also must love his wife as he loves himself, and the wife must respect her husband.

Children, obey your parents in the Lord, for this is right. "Honor your father and mother"—which is the first commandment with a promise— "so that it may go well with you and that you may enjoy long life on the earth."

I continue this series on Living an Intentional Life with a look at the family. Remember that the three key words in describing an intentional life are purpose, discipline and results. Living intentionally means that we have set the agenda for our own lives. It is not dictated by circumstances or other people. We make the decisions about how we will spend our time, energy and our resources.

I haven't done any kind of survey, but just from experience, I would bet that of all the areas of our lives that demand a block of our time, if we were to decide which was the most important, it would come down to family. I have never heard anyone say they wish they could spend less time with their family! I believe that all of the problems in our world today are the effect of a break-down in the family. ("cause and effect") and it began in the Garden of Eden.

I do not claim to have all the answers for what is ailing families today, but I can say with certainty that I can point you in the direction of the one who does! And, I can help you develop your own "Intentional Time Budget Plan" for family, that will produce the desired results you want in your life, and in your family.

The family is not a product of human ingenuity, it is an institution and a creation of God. As such, it holds a place of importance in life second only to our personal relationship with Him. If I wanted to depress you, I could run through a series of demoralizing statistics on the state of families in our country. But, that is not my intention. I want to focus on the fact that if we keep our priorities in order, and focus our time and attention on what is most important, it is possible to have a happy, healthy, abundant family life. Notice that I did not say we would have a "perfect" family life. That may be what we dream of, but we must live in the real world. It is possible however, to do the things we have always "intended" to do with our families; if we develop a "family time budget".

The amount of time is not as important as the quality. I and my wife once decided that one of the intentional family times on our calendar was going to be a special time each month with each one of our children and their families. They set the date, they choose what they would like to do, and we mark it on the calendar. It's a date! And nothing would come before that date. It is hard to do now with the distance barrier, but we could change it to once a year or whatever would work.

Well, let's look at God's suggestions for the family;

1. Wives - Ephesians 5:22-24 tell us "Wives, submit to your husbands as to the Lord. For the husband is the head of the wife as Christ is the head of the church, his body, of which he is the Savior. Now as the church submits to Christ, so also wives should submit to their husbands in everything."

Wives are to submit to their husbands. There are some men that simply like the way that sounds. But they don't understand what it means. There are also a number of ladies, who are thinking, SUBMIT? No way! I think that they too probably do not understand what these verses are saying.

It's important for us to nail this down. We must have a proper understanding of what this means. No matter what your initial reaction to that word submit, I submit to you that we cannot improve upon what God has told us in his word! If he says this is the way something should work we would do well to take heed. However, we must make sure we understand.

Paul is speaking here within the context of a Christian marriage. He is not implying that women are inferior to men in any way, or that all women should be subject to men. The very nature of the word "submit" suggests a voluntary action; a willingness; you can't force someone into submission. It is a willingness on behalf of the Christian wife to allow her husband to be what God has called him to be; the spiritual leader of the home and the head of the household. Not as a "Lord over all!" or "I am King!" kind of thing, but it must be said - this submission to the husband is only as he submits himself to God. A truly happy and fulfilling marriage is one where both husband and wife are committed to each other and their relationship with God and His desire and direction for their lives. (together!)

But, this is not a one-sided deal. Paul also says "Husbands, love your wives". I would suggest that we start by reading and re-reading 1 Corinthians 13 as many times as it takes, until we actually "get it!" Try this; (Read 1 Corinthians 13 and put your name in place of the word "love" or "it". For instance; "_____ is patient"… "_____ is never rude…" etc. Until we understand this, we will never understand what real love is!

What exactly does it mean in Ephesians 6 that Jesus "gave himself up"? It means that he submitted to the will of God, willingly. This can be illustrated by sticking a gun in someone's back; when they lift their hands into the air they have surrendered to my will. This is surrender, not submission! It says in Luke 9:51 - "As the time approached for him to be taken up to heaven, Jesus *resolutely* set out for Jerusalem". Knowing the outcome, he willingly and resolutely, set out for Jerusalem! That's submission.

This raises the stakes for us gentlemen. While many of us may secretly smile at the word submit we must understand that we are responsible for providing the atmosphere for that "willingness" to happen! Not by sticking a gun in someone's back to force them to surrender, but in the context of the fact that as we are submitted and surrendered to the will of God in our own lives; wives can willingly submit to our leadership.

Not only did Jesus give himself up, but he did it so that the church could reach its full potential and become all God had intended it to become. If we are to be men of God and heads of our homes, we must submit to God so that our wives (and our entire families for that matter) can reach their full potential and become all that God intends (them) to be. It's a win-win situation!

When we look at it this way, we can begin to understand and even accept what is given here as a blueprint for married life. The marriage commitment is one that takes time and we must make the time to make it work. We must have as a part of our "family time budget" an intentional time to spend with our spouse. Whether it's a dinner date or some other kind of time alone. It has to be a specific, intentional time that is marked on the calendar.

But, there is more; Proverbs 22:6—"**Train** a child in the way he should go, and when he is old he will not turn from it." Parents, our job is to train our children. In other words, to the best of our abilities, we are to prepare them to live responsible, productive lives in this world. And the best way to do that is to set a good example.

The primary job of children in the family is to grow, learn, and mature and have fun doing it. As they grow, children go through many changes: mentally, physically, spiritually, socially, and emotionally. In all of those things, the apostle Paul also has something to say; "Children, obey your parents in the Lord, for this is right. Honor your father and mother —which is the first commandment with a promise—that it may go well with you and that you may enjoy long life on the earth." Bill Cosby used to say "I made you and I can take you out! And, I can make another one to replace you!"

Paul tells us that such obedience to parents is an indication of their relationship with the Lord. Children are to realize that both they and their parents are under the authority of God. Paul says this is the right thing for you to do; and, there are great benefits! You will enjoy long life, and your "sit-down" won't hurt as much!

#1. The home is to be a place of unconditional love and acceptance. #2. The home is to be a place of total surrender to the word and will of God. #3. The home is to be a place of preparation where all of us learn to be godly, responsible and productive in this life. #4. The home is the center or the core of our life, and all other aspects of life radiate out from the home. The family should never be a source of stress in our lives! And, if we make the time and take the time, it can and will become less and less stressful.

That is a lot to say concerning the purposes of family life; however, no family will have a successful home life without spending time together. I know that many of us wonder where we're going to get the additional time we need for everything? Well, let me help you with that. YOU'RE NOT GETTING ANY ADDITIONAL

TIME! As I pointed out—we've all got the same amount. 24 hours a day. 168 hours a week. So, if we are not getting any more, then we need to better budget the time we have.

What do you want your family life to be? Forget about the Brady Bunch -or The Cleavers -or Ozie and Harriet. (The Nelson's) Those are families of fiction. However, if we would all submit ourselves to the Lord and take the roles he has defined for our families, we just might find that even though they never will become perfect, they sure can be better than we ever imagined. Having a great family is not something that happens by accident. It's something that the entire family works at....Intentionally!

Acts 2:42-47 – "They devoted themselves to the apostles' teaching and to fellowship, to the breaking of bread and to prayer. Everyone was filled with awe at the many wonders and signs performed by the apostles. All the believers were together and had everything in common. They sold property and possessions to give to anyone who had need. Every day they continued to meet together in the temple courts. They broke bread in their homes and ate together with glad and sincere hearts, praising God and enjoying the favor of all the people. And the Lord added to their number daily those who were being saved."

Remember an intentional life is one with purpose. The purpose is followed with a bold and steady determination until the desired outcome is realized. In other words, an intentional life has three foundational characteristics—purpose, discipline and results. So far, we have looked at an intentional spiritual life and intentional family life. Now, I want to pursue a topic that is actually an ingredient of our spiritual lives — but not the same…church.

By looking at this portion of the Book of Acts, perhaps we can discover our purpose in the church—What are we here for?

A. Teaching—"They devoted themselves to the apostles' teaching." The focal point of the church is the Word of God. Everything we do is governed by this book. Our preaching, our Sunday school and Bible study. Romans chapter ten tells us that "faith comes by hearing the word." This is true, however, our faith grows and matures in **response** to the Word of God. Notice that I said growth and maturity takes place **in response to** the Word. It is not enough to sit through a sermon, or to listen to or participate in a Bible study. The word must be acted upon and put into practice. James chapter one tells us that if we fail to do what the word says we deceive ourselves. Is there some area of this purpose of the church in which you could be a part? (B.) Belonging—"They devoted themselves; to the fellowship." The church is a place where everyone belongs. In other words, it is a place where everyone is welcome. The church is to be a place with open arms. We accept everyone because God accepts us. We love everyone because God loves us. We forgive everyone because God forgives us. Church should provide a sense that says, "I belong to – or am a part of something bigger than myself" and it's not about me!

When I went off to Indiana to be "paper trained" (take ordination classes) I quickly found people with whom I had something in common. I found people who were pastors in churches just like me. Even though these people were not from my home town, or from my home state, there was a sense of the familiar. We had a common bond that supported us miles from home. We were no longer isolated individuals out on our own, we were part of a fellowship; a fellowship of believers. We became friends because we were all a part of something bigger than ourselves. I was not just the pastor of a church in northern Wisconsin; I was part of something greater than that; I was part of God's church; the fellowship of those who are saved, called, and delivered, and sent to carry a message to the world.

Church should do the same for everyone who walks through our doors. We are all different people with different backgrounds, lives, personalities, family make-up, and so on, but when we gather together, we understand that though we are different, none of us is alone in serving God. There are others; our church is a team; a part of a world-wide team, with God as the owner - the Holy Spirit as manager - and Jesus as coach! We all belong to the family of God and it is bigger...much bigger...than any individual. Is there any way that you can think of that you could intentionally be a part of this purpose of the church?

(C.) Worshipping—"They devoted themselves...to the breaking of bread" This would be a meal that believers shared together and more often than not would include what we now call communion; a symbol of worship and remembrance.

Church is a place where God is worshipped. That worship can take many forms. We can sing hymns, we can sing choruses, we can stand, we can sit, we can be loud and clap our hands, or we can be silent. The form or style of worship is not nearly as important as the object of our worship—God himself. This is truly the reason we gather on Sunday mornings; and the only reason; to worship God. To pray to Him; to listen to His Word and hear Him speak; but, most of all to offer our worship and praise in remembrance of what he has done in our lives. Everything the church does should be an act of worship! Can you be a part of worship? Can you make worship an intentional part of your life?

(D.) Praying—"They devoted themselves...to prayer." When Jesus cleansed the temple of those who were using it for profit he said, "My house will be called a house of prayer, but you are making it a den of robbers."

The church is a house of prayer because it is understood that it is a place where people come to meet God. It is true that Scripture teaches that the Holy Spirit lives in each of us and that we are his temples, but the church is still a place recognized for God's presence.

We must be careful that the church is not only understood as a place to meet God, but that it is also a place where God is able to change lives! This is why we have things like: a prayer bowl of concerns; this is why we meet twice a month for "Circles of Prayer"; this is why we have prayer several times during our worship service. God is in the business of changing and transforming lives, and we are in the business of prayer! Can you be a prayer partner? Could Prayer become an intentional part of your ministry in the church?

(E.) Ministering—and Ministry - "Everyone was filled with awe, and many wonders and miraculous signs were done by the apostles. All the believers were together and had everything in common. Selling their possessions and goods, they gave to anyone as he had need." (vv. 43-45)

In Ephesians 4, the apostle Paul listed one of the primary objectives of ministry as "preparing God's people for works of service." This means that God never intended for the pastor and his family to monopolize the ministry opportunities in the church. The church is not a place for only sitting, it is a place for service. It is where we learn what gifts the Lord has given us and how we can use them to build his kingdom through His local body.

We've already seen that the church is here to teach the Word, help people to belong, worship God, pray and minister; so what does all of that have to do with me? The answer is simple: The church must be a part of our intentional living plan. It must have a place in our time budget.

Intentional time to meet with God; intentional time to communicate with God in prayer; intentional time to worship God as Creator, Sustainer, and Savior of mankind; intentional time to serve Him in one of the many ways possible in the church; Intentional time to do those things concerning the church which we have allowed circumstances, people, family, and friends, and fishing and golfing and whatever else dictate our time and set our agenda.

If the church is here to teach the word of God; come expecting to be taught and to learn! God wants to communicate with you. Pray that God would communicate with you. Ask him to help your heart and mind be open. Ask him to help you understand. Pray that God will clearly communicate with everyone else as well.

If the church is here to help people belong…Come and be the first one with a smile and a warm greeting. Take time to get to know the people in the church. Talk to them here; and spend time with them away from here.

If the church is a place to worship God; come and set the example for people around you. People are watching you whether you like it or not. Some people come and stand in church and their whole attitude during worship screams the title of the hymn I SHALL NOT BE MOVED! You, as an individual, are important to the atmosphere of worship in our church. It doesn't matter if you are outwardly expressive or more reserved. The issue is that you take advantage of the opportunity to worship God with sincere expression, and with other people who love him too.

IF the church is a place for prayer; take the chance to pray and have your faith encouraged by a group of people who gather in a place dedicated to providing an atmosphere in which you can freely communicate with God. Take the time to pray for yourself, your family and the other people who are around you. Perhaps you could help set the tone by praying at the beginning of each service for God's blessings and His will to be done in the service.

If the church is a place for ministry; come, and get involved. There are many, many areas of ministry in which your gifts and talents can be used! Understand that if you know Jesus as your savior, you are a prime candidate to be involved in the ministry of the church. Your job may not be on the platform, but in fact, right now, there are people in the nursery who are 'ministering' (which means serving) by provided care for the children who are here; there are those who are involved with bulletin boards and banners. Ask God to help you understand where you fit into the ministry of the church. Take the time to get **intentionally** involved.

What do you want to be when you grow up? We can ask the same question about the church. What do we envision for this place we call church, as we submit ourselves to God and his leading? Your ideas are needed! Your opinion is welcome!

I have given you a lot of things to think about concerning the church, but I want you to apply some of these things intentionally to the area of your church life. Why? Because you are needed to make the church become what God INTENDS for it to be! Will you join me in that adventure today?

Colossians 4:2-6 – "Devote yourselves to prayer, being watchful and thankful. And pray for us, too, that God may open a door for our message, so that we may proclaim the mystery of Christ, for which I am in chains. Pray that I may proclaim it clearly, as I should. Be wise in the way you act toward outsiders; make the most of every opportunity. Let your conversation be always full of grace, seasoned with salt, so that you may know how to answer everyone."

Matthew chapter 28 records these words of Jesus "go and make disciples of all nations, baptizing them in the name of the Father and of the Son and of the Holy Spirit, and teaching them to obey everything I have commanded you. And surely I am with you always, to the very end of the age." This is a process we often refer to as witnessing or evangelism. It means telling people about Jesus —and what He has done in your life; something most Christians believe they should do, but rarely ever accomplish.

Why is that? If witnessing is such an important task (and it is), why do we have such a hard time with it? Notice I use the word we. Pastors aren't some kind of Christian super heroes. This is an area that is also difficult for me a lot of times. Our difficulty stems from a number of reasons, including but not limited to: fear and uncertainty about what to say or do. This morning, I want to help us understand our role as a witness, and hopefully, in the process, we will be able to let go of the pressure and anxiety that often accompany us causing spiritual stress. Remembering that intentional living means having PURPOSE, DISCIPLINE and RESULTS, let's look at being an intentional witness.

First, the purpose of witness. A witness is one who gives testimony concerning something they have seen or experienced *first hand*. This means that the only people who can give testimony about Jesus are those who have actually had a personal experience with Him.

A witness is intended to shed personal light on the work of God in the world. We cannot operate on a purely theoretical basis—we must give flesh and blood to the Bible. It's one thing for a person to hear that Jesus can change lives; it's something totally different for family, friends, and coworkers to see the fruit of a life Jesus has changed.

Second, what are the benefits of being a witness? If you were to witness a crime and then testify in court concerning your experience, you would be described as performing your civic duty. A Christian witness could technically be described in much the same way. By testifying, you would be performing your spiritual duty. However, if we look at this issue only in terms of duty, we will miss the essence of what God is trying to do. God is more concerned about the process of our lives than He is with the product. This means that He is not primarily interested in what we do for Him but in what we become in Him. (What we become in Him will define what we do for Him.) If you have been living an unintentional life, I could ask the Dr. Phil question – "How that working for you?" Relating this to the idea of witness, we find that it is not a duty to be performed, but a privilege to be enjoyed. Just think, the Bible says "nothing is impossible for God." That means he could make this whole idea of witnessing disappear with a snap of his fingers. He could make everyone serve him if he wanted to. But, since he is more concerned with the process, he wants to allow us the opportunity to have a part in His work in the world. Therefore, the major blessing in being a witness is found in the fact that God chooses to use us!

Third, what about the discipline required to be a witness? Part of Discipline has to do with the "what" and "how" of an issue. Specifically, what should I do and how should it be done? There are a lot of good books on how to be a witness; however, I would like to give you a very simple approach to being a witness. It is found in the passage of Scripture from Colossians chapter four. I believe this passage gives us two insights into the life of an intentional witness. There is a close relationship between our witness and our spiritual lives; remember, I said a witness is one who gives testimony about something seen or experienced firsthand. However, there is this funny little thing that affects what we experience—it is called **time**. The more time that passes after an event, the fuzzier the details seem to become.

Since the passage of time affects and even softens experience for us, it is imperative that our experience with God be up-to-date, current and fresh. Paul addresses this idea by telling us to be devoted to prayer. In that devotion, he says we should be watchful and thankful. The Greek word translated watchful literally means keeping awake. Now, Paul is not primarily addressing the issue of sleepiness in prayer, he is saying "keep it alive, keep it fresh, not boring and mechanical." Keep your experience with God alive and up-to date. If I were to ask "What is God doing in your life this week?" How would you answer? It just doesn't cut it to tell me about something God did twenty years ago! What is He doing now?

By asking the Colossians to pray for him, Paul is showing us the value of praying for others. Prayer is not a selfish exercise. In fact, most of the benefit of prayer comes in the fact that we are focusing on something or someone else. By the way, when you are praying, pray for others that they too may be an effective, intentional witness.

Next, Paul tells us is to use wisdom in being a witness. He specifically addresses two areas - how we treat people and how we communicate with them. "Be wise in the way you act toward outsiders." I don't want to sound rude or judgmental here, but I can only think of one effective way to say this; don't you just want to crawl under a rock at times when people claiming to be Christians act like total idiots in public—especially those who gain media attention? Sometimes I just want to yell for everyone to hear "WE'RE NOT LIKE THAT!" I heard Jessie DuPlantis (a T.V. preacher) say once that "the way some people drive, he wished they would take the "fish" symbol off their car!" Sometimes people have a lot of zeal, but little or no wisdom.

In being wise, Paul tells us to make the most of every opportunity. When I think of opportunities, I think of open doors Paul mentioned in verse three. Most of us are wise (or should I say smart?) enough to recognize when a door is open, but Paul says, when a door is open, take the opportunity to be a witness.   However, there are two sides to that coin. The reverse would also be true: if the door is closed - keep your mouth shut - and pray and wait for it to open. Don't force the issue. There are some Christians who approach every door with a battering ram—even the ones that are open! While they may get in, it's also true that they could do a lot of damage and may even ensure that the door is never opened again. Paul says to use wisdom. If you have prayed for an open door, God will make sure you can tell it's open…"wait upon the Lord"!

Paul finishes up by giving us three characteristics of wise communication: "graciousness", "appropriateness" and "relevance": (a.) Communicate with grace. That means to be kind, courteous, tactful, merciful, compassionate, etc. The tone you use can determine whether or not the door stays open. The tone of our voice says more than the words we speak.

(b.) Communicate in an appropriate manner. Paul says that our conversation should be seasoned with salt. "Seasoned" - That means I will not empty the entire shaker onto my plate. That would ruin the meal.

(c.) Communicate in a relevant manner. One of the outstanding beauties of God's creation is that he made us all to be different. That means we will need to use a variety of means to reach a variety of people. The Apostle Paul said it this way: "I have become all things to all men that I may win some!" If I were to ask, our young people, "What goes through your mind when you think about the end of your life?" I would be totally off base because they are not thinking that their lives will end, they are thinking "I've got my life ahead of me". We need to meet people where they are. Jesus talked about fishing to fisherman, farming to farmers, and about God to religious leaders. If we can't communicate in a relevant manner, our witness will not be heard or understood or even accepted.

Here are just a few final thoughts on being an effective witness:

A. Be yourself—remember, there are no Super Hero Christians, only ordinary people like me and you.

B. Be up-to-date in your experience with God.

C. Be devoted to prayer and claim the promise written in James1:5— "If any of you lacks wisdom, he should ask God, who gives generously to all without finding fault, and it will be given to him." Trust God to help you know when a door is open and how to appropriately respond.

D. Let go of the fear, anxiety and stress that plagues us spiritually. Being a witness is not a one-shot chance at success, but a lifelong journey of adventure that allows us to be used by God's in ways we've never imagined. Perhaps we have put it off long enough! Maybe it's time to get that book or attend that class. Maybe it's time to be an Intentional Witness!

We need to ask ourselves; "Can I really do something effectively for God? Does he really want to use me? How long have I been a Christian? Do I have a story to tell? Or is my experience with God faded with time? Have I ever prayed for God to give me an "open door"? God wants to use you! Are you willing to be an intentional witness for him?

Joshua 24:14-18 – "Now fear the LORD and serve him with all faithfulness. Throw away the gods your ancestors worshiped beyond the Euphrates River and in Egypt, and serve the LORD. But if serving the LORD seems undesirable to you, then choose for yourselves this day whom you will serve, whether the gods your ancestors served beyond the Euphrates, or the gods of the Amorites, in whose land you are living. But as for me and my household, we will serve the LORD."

Then the people answered, "Far be it from us to forsake the LORD to serve other gods! It was the LORD our God himself who brought us and our parents up out of Egypt, from that land of slavery, and performed those great signs before our eyes. He protected us on our entire journey and among all the nations through which we traveled. And the LORD drove out before us all the nations, including the Amorites, who lived in the land. We too will serve the LORD, because he is our God."

There is an old story that is probably familiar to most of you. A man was walking down a country road when he heard a clatter, followed by a splash, followed by sputtered cries for help. He ran up the road and over the bank, down to a small river. He grabbed a boy of about ten years old, by his shirttail and arm as he was about to go under for the proverbial third time and pulled him up onto the riverbank. He thumped the boy on the back a few times, until he gave a couple of great coughs and began to breathe properly. They both lay there for a few moments, catching their breath. After a couple of minutes had passed, the man asked the boy "How did you come to fall in the river?" The lad replied, "I didn't come to fall in the river, I came to fish!"

In that simple exchange is great wisdom about the meaning of the word "intentional." Have you ever gone to one of life's rivers to fish, only to find yourself floundering around, over your head and going down for the third time?

Leading an intentional life is a three-part process of Purpose, to which is applied Discipline, producing Results...

Joshua 24 gives us that same story on a much larger scale. Joshua is old now, and wants one last talk with the people about God. He recalls for them how God worked in the lives of Abraham, Isaac, and Jacob, how he brought them out of Egypt, to the Promised Land, giving it to them on a silver platter, as it were. Now he comes to what he really wanted to say, the rest has just been background; vs. 14-15. - "Now fear the LORD and serve him with all faithfulness. Throw away the gods your forefathers worshipped beyond the River and in Egypt, and serve the LORD. But if serving the LORD seems undesirable to you, then choose for yourselves this day whom you will serve, whether the gods your fore-fathers served beyond the River, or the gods of the Amorites, in whose land you are living. *But as for me and my household, we will serve the LORD.*"

Joshua tells the people "You will have to choose – these are your choices - I personally have chosen - But, what will you do?" The people respond that they choose God, and he cautions them that it is not going to be easy, they could even end up on the riverbank, gasping for air. They reply, "No, we will serve the LORD."

Beautiful scene, isn't it. They had wonderful **intentions** and the **results** would have been tremendous, If only...they had found a plan in which to discipline themselves. There are no sadder words than "It might have been." Because we know the results that ultimately came of this moment, we can see what "might have been". The people had no discipline, a failing that could not be overcome even by the best of their intentions.

The focus in this lesson is "choose for yourselves this day whom you will serve."

We tend to concentrate on the "big issues" of life whenever we seek to figure out how we came to be in such a pickle, or how we came to be so stressed out and strung out like a tight rubber band. But, it is really the day-to-day decisions we make that dictate our "big issues." We are going to look at four areas of our personal lives where many a person's stated purpose is at odds with the level of discipline they are willing to practice, leading to unsatisfactory results.

The first area we will discuss is that of our Tithes. I am not going to tell you that you need to give more, that you are robbing God, or that you are denying yourselves the blessings that God is waiting to pour out on you. I don't need to tell you any of those things because you've heard them before …you already know these things…and my text is not from Malachi. I am certainly not going to tell you how much you need to give, because, hopefully God has told you that. If you are a Christian, it should at least be your **intention to give**.

I just want to ask you two simple questions – "Is it your purpose to honor God in your financial life?" Are your results demonstrating that purpose, or are they showing that discipline is lacking? If your intent is to give honor to God through your finances, then your discipline will be to live your life in such a way that, gives God the glory for blessing and providing for you as you seek to be vessels through which He can reach this world for Christ. As 1st Corinthians 9:7 says, "Each man should give what he has decided in his heart to give, not reluctantly or under compulsion, for God loves a cheerful giver." I heard of a church where – every time the pastor would announce it was time to take the offering, the people would literally stand up and cheer like they were at a football game!

What goes into that discipline? – a hundred little decisions every day, questions that have nothing to do with what we have... and everything to do with what we do with what we have and what we are willing to give.

It does not matter how much or how little you have – if your purpose is to honor God, then your intentional discipline demands that God come first in your checkbook, and the results will demonstrate it in your life in ways that you can't even imagine!

Our second area of emphasis is our time. Ecclesiastes 4:4-6 tells us much about time, and a little about money as well. "And I saw that all labor and all achievement spring from man's envy of his neighbor. This too is meaningless, a chasing after the wind. 'The fool folds his hands and ruins himself. Better one handful with tranquility than two handfuls with toil and chasing after the wind."

Two extremes are presented here. The Teacher condemns the fool who does nothing to take care of himself or his family, and in the next sentence condemns the workaholic – What will it take to please this guy? Obviously, the answer is the man who does enough for himself and his family yet keeps his eyes on the truly important things, which he terms "one handful with tranquility."

The question, once again, is what do you intend to do with your time? And again, those around you might have a truer picture than you do. If your intention is to use your time in a godly fashion, then the results should bear that out. Is it your purpose to raise a godly family? Then you won't be working 60-70 hours a week. Is it your purpose to know God and His Word? Then you won't spend every evening parked in front of the TV while your Bible gathers dust and the knees of your pants show no wear! A hundred little decisions, each day, the seemingly meaningless choices of daily life, will once again make the big decisions for you. There will come a time when you will reflect on your life and all the things you "intended" to do, but didn't.

Another part of life that requires discipline to live out our intentions is our talents. Acts 11:27-29 tells of a time of need in the Church, and how the disciples met that need - "During this time some prophets came down from Jerusalem to Antioch. One of them, named Agabus, stood up and through the Spirit predicted that a severe famine would spread over the entire Roman world. (This happened during the reign of Claudius.) The disciples, *each according to his ability*, decided to provide help for the brothers living Judea."

The disciples made use of their abilities, or talents, to help someone else. Their intention was to do what they could do, for the benefit of someone else. What is your intention or purpose for the abilities you have been given? Do you even see yourself as talented? Everyone has God-given, *self-ignored*, talents. Why do we do that? Ignore our talents? Some of us have talents and abilities that we don't even see as being talents or abilities! And we ignore them.

Sometimes out of fear, we are like the man with one talent in Matthew 25 who knew, he just knew, that he couldn't do anything with that one talent, so he was going to keep that thing a secret, you know, just between himself and God, because it just wouldn't do as much as the five talents the other man received; it wasn't as noticeable or great; it was just one little talent.

Sometimes we dismiss our talents because we just don't care. In the Parable of the Good Samaritan, it is quite possible that the priest and the Levite had a greater ability to help the wounded man than the Samaritan did – if nothing else, they were there and in position to render aid sooner; even that would have been better than just walking by. However, their intention was not to be useful and loving, but to be holy and dignified. Or maybe they were just saving their talents for a better time, or someone more worthy of their efforts. You and I both know that they would not have walked by on the other side of the road if they had seen that the injured man was a fellow Temple worker. What is the purpose of your God-given talents? Are you disciplining your life so that you can exercise them for the Kingdom?

Someone may be thinking, "You sure are misreading that Acts passage!" What it means is that they gave as much money as they could afford, that's what it means." Yep! And while generosity is a talent, the ability to see needs and know how to use what God has given you to meet them is an even greater talent.

The final area is temperament. What is your temperament? Do you meet the qualifications of a deacon or an overseer, as given in I Timothy 3? Or would those who know you compare you to Nabal, whose name meant fool, and whose beautiful, talented wife it is said lived up, or perhaps I should say down, to his name. Perhaps you resemble Ishmael, who's mother was told by the Angel of the LORD that he would be a "wild donkey of a man," living in perpetual hostility toward all around him. Ecclesiastes 4 gave us the opposing pictures of the lazy man sitting with his hands folded, and the grasping workaholic. Which of these describes you? Does it match with your intentions?

Some may regard their temperament as fixed, the product of genetics and environment – bunk! To that I say two things – **Free Will**. Telling the LORD that I was an alcoholic, thieving, wife-beater because I come from a long line of alcoholic, thieving, wife-beaters may make it on the psychiatrist's couch, but it will not hold water when you stand before the LORD! Each man dies for his own sin, because he has made his own decisions. Keep in mind that this works both ways – you cannot draw water from the well of a godly upbringing very long before the well runs dry and you are left with what **you** really are.

II Corinthians 5:17 - "Therefore, if anyone is in Christ, he is a new creation; the old has gone, the new has come!" If it is your intention to serve Christ, then get out of the way, so he can change your temperament! I'm reminded of Romans 12:2 which says "Do not be conformed any longer to the pattern of this world, but be transformed by the renewing of your mind" (the way you think about things) "Then you will be able to test and approve what God's will is; His good, pleasing and perfect will."

All of our decisions interact, you know. All I have to do to illustrate that is to give the example of a place near our home in Wisconsin..."Hole in the Wall." It's a Casino. A good place to waste your time and money, while letting your talents rust and your temperament be changed to either anger or despair.

So, Joshua proposes the question; "Choose for yourselves this day whom you will serve, whether the gods your forefathers served beyond the River, or the gods of the Amorites, in whose land you are living. But as for me and my house, we will serve the LORD."

The gods they had served in Egypt are like the past; holding onto us and saying "if only". The gods of the Amorites are the temptations we will have to overcome today, they are the "maybe we can" or "maybe we should" or "maybe we shouldn't" of life. Joshua states that he will live in the present with the intention this day to discipline his life and to INTENTIONALLY serve the LORD. How about you? What will you do in these areas of Tithe, Time, Talents, and Temperament?

Colossians 3:23-24 – "Whatever you do, work at it with all your heart, as working for the Lord, not for human masters, since you know that you will receive an inheritance from the Lord as a reward. It is the Lord Christ you are serving."

2 Peter 1:3-15 – "His divine power has given us everything we need for a godly life through our knowledge of him who called us by his own glory and goodness. Through these he has given us his very great and precious promises, so that through them you may participate in the divine nature, having escaped the corruption in the world caused by evil desires.

For this very reason, make every effort to add to your faith goodness; and to goodness, knowledge; and to knowledge, self-control; and to self-control, perseverance; and to perseverance, godliness; and to godliness, mutual affection; and to mutual affection, love. For if you possess these qualities in increasing measure, they will keep you from being ineffective and unproductive in your knowledge of our Lord Jesus Christ. But whoever does not have them is nearsighted and blind, forgetting that they have been cleansed from their past sins.

Therefore, my brothers and sisters, make every effort to confirm your calling and election. For if you do these things, you will never stumble, and you will receive a rich welcome into the eternal kingdom of our Lord and Savior Jesus Christ."

During this teaching, we have seen the fact that God has always worked in an intentional manner—that is, He has a purpose and a plan for everyone. He has given certain gifts and abilities and talents to everyone. He has also given us freewill to choose whether or not we will "seek it, find it, and do it" especially when it comes to His plan for abundant living.

We've have considered the benefits of living intentionally in our spiritual lives, family lives, church life, personal life, and in our call to be an intentional witness. In the broader scope of things, we may ask; "Are there any benefits to this idea?" If you are tired of never seeming to do what you feel is important in your life, then my answer is an emphatic "YES!"

I believe this question can be answered in the premise I gave you in the beginning... "If we do not have an agenda for our lives, one will be provided for us—either by circumstances, or by other people." Intentional Living means that we are taking control and determining how we will live our lives and spend our time, our energy and our resources. Without such a plan, life can easily "get away from us" and because we never accomplish those things that are most important in our lives we live with stress in our families, stress at work, stress with our finances, stress in every area we have discussed.

We should never be so sure of ourselves and our ability to always do exactly what God desires. We are a fallen people and given the opportunity we will fall still farther. That's why intentional living is such an important issue. "If we always do what we have always done; we will always get what we have always got!"

The reason I have put this Intentional Living Plan together is because I think there are many Christians in our churches today who are "sea-sick"! Seasickness is motion sickness. There are many people who wish the world would just stop for a while so they can catch their breath and catch up. Most of those people have lives filled with activity for which there is no clear cut purpose. They often become disoriented, distressed and sometimes even become physically sick due the constant motion of their lives which has no purpose. We need an anchor! An anchor makes sure that the motion can only go so far before we are drawn back. Living intentional and on purpose lives is a guide to keep us on course and ensure we are focusing on the right things.

There is a story involving Yogi Berra, the well-known catcher for the New York Yankees, and Hank Aaron, who at the time was the chief power hitter for the Milwaukee Braves. The teams were playing in the World Series, and as usual Yogi was keeping up his ceaseless chatter intended to pep up his team-mates and distract the Milwaukee batters. As Aaron came to the plate, Yogi tried to distract him by saying, "Henry, can't you read? You're holding the bat wrong. You're supposed to hold it so you can read the trademark." Aaron didn't say anything. When the next pitch came he hit a homerun into the left field bleachers. After rounding the bases and reaching home plate, Aaron looked at Yogi and said, "I didn't come up here to read."

Knowing your purpose helps keep you on track. It allows you to ignore the things that can easily distract you and take your attention away from the things that really matter in your life.

It has been rightly said that "good is the enemy of the best." There are many people who have had and done good things in life, and they say that they have had a "good" life....but they have never known life in all its fullness. They have never experienced the abundant life. The life of having balance in the eight areas of life we have discussed. The problem with most of us is not that we haven't had opportunity; it's that we lack discipline.

There is, of course, great benefit in discipline. By discipline I do not mean punishment or correction. Rather, I am talking about the self-control it takes to do the right things. All of us have had many good intentions about doing the things that matter most in our lives. But, we have always allowed "this" and "that" to take up our time. When we discipline ourselves to an intentional time budget, and actually mark it on the calendar, and then just do it; we take control.

Discipline helps you do the right things and get the best results. Discipline is what makes a gold medal winner a winner! It's like the saying I once heard a preacher use—THE MAIN THING IS TO KEEP THE MAIN THING THE MAIN THING. It's like the movie "The City Slickers"- In the movie the rugged old cowboy tells Billy Crystal that the secret to his peace in life was finding that "one thing!" In other words, invest your time, energy and resources on the right things in your life, and the return, or the reward, will be more than you imagined.

Have you ever noticed that it's often easier to live a shallow life than to deal with it on a deeper level? It reminds me of a swimming pool. There is a shallow end and a deep end. Many people like to live life in the shallow end because the risk is minimal. The problem is that a person is limited in what they can do there. However, some feel it's a good trade to not have to deal with the uncertainty and danger of the deep end. I have a book in my library by Chuck Swindol called; "Living Above The Level Of Mediocrity" that would be a great book to read as it concerns a "commitment to excellence". When In search of the abundant life he would say; "Live in the deep end!"

Life is a risk. To confront the risk brings greater reward, satisfaction and fulfillment than staying in the shallow end ever will. Let me say one last thing about the shallow end—the one major crisis we have all heard about in pools happens in the shallow end. Someone decides to dive in head first and hits his head on the bottom. In some cases this has proved to be disastrous. But the trauma occurred when *someone tried to do something in the shallow end that was not possible there.* If he had gone to the deep end, he could have completed his dive and come up with the thrill and satisfaction of accomplishment.

M. Scott Peck writes in his book "The Road Less Traveled" - "I spent much of my ninth summer on a bicycle. About a mile from our house the road went down a steep hill and turned sharply at the bottom. Coasting down the hill one morning, I felt my gathering speed to be ecstatic. To give up this ecstasy by applying brakes seemed an absurd self-punishment. So I resolved to simultaneously retain my speed and negotiate the corner. My ecstasy ended seconds later when I was propelled a dozen feet off the road into the woods. I was badly scratched and bleeding, and the front wheel of my new bike was twisted beyond use from its impact against a tree. I had been unwilling to suffer the pain of giving up my ecstatic speed in the interest of maintaining my balance around the corner. I learned, however, that the loss of balance is ultimately more painful."

The point is that there are some people who seem to focus only on one area of their lives - such as (physical health) or (recreation- - leisure) making sure they allot special time to those areas…usually at the expense of all the other areas.

The problem of course, is that there is *stress* in the imbalance, and these people usually opt for pleasure rather than pain. So, when the wife starts to complain about the fact that they are always out playing golf rather than doing what needs to be done around the house; the next thing you know, they are in divorce court! When there is stress at work, they go from job to job. When the spirit suffers, they just plain quit going to church or feeding their intellect, and so on.

However, I believe that it only makes sense, that when purpose and discipline come together in all of the areas of our lives, we begin to find balance. Balance in our time, balance in where we focus our energy, and balance in the use of our resources. Living an intentional life will lead you through life's journey with definite destinations in mind. You will be taking control of these things in your life, and stress will be replaced by happiness, peace, and a true sense of accomplishment. But, most of all, we will have found balance in our out of control lives.

I don't like to use scripture in a way that may be out of context, but there is wisdom to be found in the Book of James when I think of the application to intentional living; James 4:1-3 says "What causes fights and quarrels among you? Don't they come from your desires that battle within you? You want something but don't get it.

You kill and covet, but you cannot have what you want. You quarrel and fight. You do not have because you do not ask God. When you ask you do not receive, because you ask with wrong motives, that you may spend what you get on your pleasures". And from James 1:22-25 - "Do not merely listen to the word, and so deceive yourselves. Do what it says. Anyone who listens to the word but does not do what it says is like a man who looks at his face in a mirror, and after looking at himself, goes away and immediately forgets what he looks like. But the man who looks intently into the perfect law that gives freedom, and continues to do this, not forgetting what he has heard, but doing it - he will be blessed in what he does!"

If you haven't yet, why not start - living "INTENTIONALLY" today!

Rev. Fred is also the author of several other books including:

"In It For Life" – Tate Publishing

"By His Hand" – Crossbooks Publishing

"Show and Tell" – Life Ministries

"Jars of Clay" – Life Ministries

"The Promised Gift" – Life Ministries

"The Kingdom of God" – Life Ministries

"From the Pastor's Desk" – Life Ministries

And

"More From the Pastor's Desk"

Made in the USA
Columbia, SC
23 September 2022

67410838R00138